My Home Away from Home

Life at Perkins School for the Blind

Robert T. Branco

DLD Books

ISBN: 1482633531
ISBN-13: 978–1482633535

Table of Contents

About the Author

Robert Theodore Branco is a life-long resident of New Bedford, Massachusetts. Legally blind since birth, Robert attended "sight-saving classes" in the public school system until his parents learned of the Perkins School for the Blind.

This book tells of Robert's experiences during his eight years at the Perkins School and will provide you with an understanding of some of what life was like for a young man growing up without total vision in a sighted world.

After graduating from Perkins, Robert went on to attend Bristol Community College and then the University of Massachusetts Dartmouth. He studied Business Administration at Bristol College, earning an Associate's degree, and Finance at UMass, earning a Bachelor's degree.

Robert's working experience has been quite varied. He has been a health benefits counselor, a customer service representative, the manager of an automotive parts department, and the receptionist at a construction company.

Currently, Robert is the publisher of *The Consumer Vision Magazine* and the president of a bowling league for disabled persons.

You can reach Bob by e-mail at: branco182@verizon.net Phone: 508-994-4972

Other books by Robert T. Branco

Publication information updated December 2015. More details are at **http://www.dvorkin.com/robertbranco/**

As I See It: From a Blind Man's Perspective (2013)
Here, the author discusses a broad spectrum of topics relating to blindness, including discrimination, myths, adaptive technology, training, legislation, and more.

From Amazon: $10 in paperback, $3.99 as an e–book for Kindle.

Available in other e–book formats from Apple, Kobo, Barnes and Noble, and Smashwords.

What We Love to Eat (2012)
This is a cookbook containing recipes that were all submitted by blind contributors.

The book is available in large print, audio CD, and Braille formats.

All sales benefit The Consumer Vision Magazine.

To order in any format, please make out a check for $10 to Consumer Vision and mail it to:

Bob Branco
359 Coggeshall St.
New Bedford, MA 02746

Weighing Things Up (2014)

This is Bob Branco's fourth published book. It includes 30 essays on issues pertaining to blindness and the blind, then another 73 short essays having to do with bureaucracy, holidays, legislation, politics, sports, scams, technology, and social issues. Numerous editor's notes and links to articles add more information and occasionally a different point of view.

From Amazon: $13.95 in paperback, $3.99 as an e-book for Kindle.

Available in other e-book formats from Apple, Kobo, Barnes and Noble, and Smashwords.

Introduction

This book is about eight of the most important years of my life. Just like anyone else between the ages of 12 and 19, I had a lot to learn about growing up. However, contrary to what most pre-teens and teens experience, I lived those eight years at Perkins School for the Blind, in Watertown, Massachusetts, 65 miles from my home.

In the book, I talk about our academic classes, our teachers and other adults at the school, the many kids who became my friends and others who made friendship impossible, the several sports we pursued, all the rules we were supposed to follow and how radically they were sometimes broken, some of the fascinating field trips we took and new technology that we explored, the ways in which the school tried to prepare us for independent living, and much more. As you will read, there were plenty of both good and bad times.

It is also important to note that I was at Perkins during the entire directorship of the only visually impaired chief administrator Perkins ever had, Mr. Ben Smith. My classmates and I watched in almost unanimous approval as he changed many of the school's long-lasting policies.

I decided to write this book because I continuously tell my friends about my adventures during those years, and I used to kid around that I could write a book, because there was so much information for me to share. Finally, I took the plunge and decided to write my experiences down, so I could share them with the world.

I hope that my story puts a unique perspective on what it's like for any teenager, blind or sighted, to live away from home for eight years. I certainly hope that the sighted, as well as the blind, will enjoy and appreciate my story.

I would like to thank my editor, Leonore H. Dvorkin, for working closely with me. I am grateful to her for completely understanding both the nature and the aim of this book. See the end of the book for more about the editing and publishing services that she and her husband offer.

I would also like to thank Ross Chartoff for his role in helping me to assemble and submit the required components of this book.

Bob Branco
New Bedford, Massachusetts
February 2013

Chapter 1

Preparation and Evaluation

For the first five years of my education, I attended a sight-saving class in my city, New Bedford, Massachusetts. In the 1960s, sight-saving classes were quite popular. Children with visual impairments would be in the same classroom with one another, and where the class sizes were so small, the kids received a lot of individual attention. The teacher tried her best to work with the students, knowing the situation that each of us had to deal with.

Of all the students in the sight-saving class, I probably needed more attention than the others, only because I couldn't read the large-print material that was available for everyone else. Though I had usable travel vision — that is, enough vision for getting around — I couldn't read the printed text. As a result, a Braille tutor came to my class for one hour each day in order to teach me Braille. I would bring my school desk out into the corridor with my tutor, and we would work on the Braille alphabet first. Then we progressed to Grade Two Braille, Braille math, and other accessible tools, including tactile maps for learning geography.

You're probably wondering how I spent the rest of my

school day without my Braille tutor. The regular teacher tried her best to include me in what the other students were working on, but she was limited in what she could do because I couldn't read print. However, once I had learned Braille, and because I was able to get Braille copies of the same reading books that my classmates had, I was included in some of the reading lessons, as I could follow along. During those times when the teacher didn't include me in the lessons, I spent time practicing Braille, coloring, or doing other projects.

I found my school experience quite rewarding, and for several years, I enjoyed the routine of getting up in the morning, having breakfast, taking the bus to school, spending the day with my classmates, and then riding home on the bus.

In the winter of 1969, my parents were informed that the State of Massachusetts could no longer accommodate me at my school. I was 11 years old at the time, and did not ask too many questions about what my parents were told. However, my mother informed me that I might have to leave home and attend a private school for the blind. Needless to say, my parents and I were against the decision, but we knew that in order for me to continue with my education, we'd have to abide by it. I was so involved in my school routine and in my home life that it had never occurred to me that it could all come to an abrupt end. I simply went through the motions. Likewise, when I had to do something in preparation for my new life at the private school, I simply went along with it.

By March of 1969, it was practically a done deal. In September, I would be going to the Perkins School for the Blind in Watertown, Massachusetts. All I knew about Perkins was that blind children of all ages went there, and that they had to live on campus if it was too far for them to go home in the evenings. I would have to live on campus and come home on weekends, because Perkins was 65 miles away.

Once everyone had agreed upon and accepted this decision,

including my parents, my Braille tutor, and my teacher, plans were made to introduce me to life at Perkins. On Sunday, March 23, 1969, my mother, my tutor, and my teacher took me to the Perkins annual Open House, where the students would participate in academic and extracurricular activities to show the general public what the school was like.

The Open House took place in the main classroom building, and the tour took approximately one hour. We observed blind children reading English, reading a foreign language, making arts and crafts, working in the wood and metal shops, performing physical education exercises, swimming, sewing, playing games, and more. For anyone who didn't know that blind children could do such things, it was a real education. My mother, even though she was trying to hide her tears at the prospect of my going to live at Perkins several months from then, was happy to see what the school did for its children. The Open House was the primary example of that.

The next step was to find the right fit for me in a Perkins classroom. On Tuesday, April 29, 1969, my mother and my Braille tutor drove me to Perkins, where I would spend the day at school. In my opinion, the reason was twofold. I think that the Perkins school principal needed to find out what grade to assign me to in the fall, while at the same time, I would be introduced to the Perkins routine.

When I arrived on campus, I was taken to the sixth-grade classroom and participated in whatever the lesson was for that day. Though the teacher and the students were very nice and respectful, I felt uneasy, both because this was a brand-new experience and because I knew that this experience was not a one-shot deal. This was going to be my life for the foreseeable future.

After spending one hour in the classroom, I had lunch in one of the cottages where the boys lived, Potter Cottage. I met the housemother in charge, and I was taken to the dining room, where she picked out a chair for me. There was a boy on each side of me, and the housemother introduced me to them. I was thinking, *Who knows? These boys could be two of my best friends someday.*

After lunch, I was taken to the playground outside of Potter Cottage. The boys had a brief recess before they began their afternoon school session, so many took advantage of the free time by playing on the seesaw, swinging on the swings, roller skating on the skating rink, or bowling. I decided to bowl with one of the boys. The bowling lane consisted of two long wooden sides, and in the back were 10 bowling pins, which we were taught to arrange ourselves. We were able to do that because below each pin was a large, tactile marble dot indicating where the pin should go. The wooden sides were erected in case the bowling ball didn't go straight down the lane. The ball would bounce off one of the sides and head back for the pins.

After bowling, it was time to go home. Afterwards, I didn't spend too much time thinking about my experience during my evaluation, and I didn't wonder where the school principal would assign me in the fall. I wasn't thinking that far ahead. All I knew was that the next day I would be back in my sight–saving class, continuing with the routine that I knew and enjoyed.

Two days after my evaluation, I came home from school only to be informed that I had to go for a blood test. In the back of my mind, I knew it had something to do with my preparation for Perkins, but once it was over, I didn't give it much thought.

Chapter 2

Welcome to Perkins School

Throughout the remainder of the spring of 1969 and into the summer, I lived life from day to day, doing the things that I enjoyed. In late June, I spent my very last day in the sight–saving class, knowing full well that I was going to a new school in September. I knew it in my head, but I was too busy enjoying life to know it in my heart. My mother and I tried to avoid the subject as much as possible, unless there was a need to bring it up.

For example, the housemothers at Perkins wanted the children's clothing to be labeled with their names, so that each article of clothing could be identified. My mother had to make up the labels and sew them to the articles of clothing. We had to discuss where the labels were located, particularly on pants, shirts, socks, galoshes, etc. At times, my mother and I also discussed other items I should take with me to Perkins, things with which I could pass the time, such as crayons and paper to draw on. Little did we know that there wasn't going to be enough time at Perkins for me to dabble in coloring.

Two weeks before it was time for me to leave home and go to Perkins, the reality of it all set in, and I did a lot of crying when I realized that I wouldn't continue to live life the way I was used to. I tried not to mention why I was so sad, but I'm sure it was obvious to my mother and everyone else. Then I started to think about my new life. What kind of friends would I meet? Would the housemothers be like my real mother? Would the teachers be as nice as the ones from the sight–saving class in New Bedford? However, I knew that I would be living in Potter Cottage with a lot of other boys, so I felt I'd make friends quickly.

On Sunday afternoon, September 7, 1969, I walked out of my house with my mom and several other relatives, suitcase in hand, as we prepared for the drive to Perkins School. The one consolation I felt at that moment was that I wouldn't be staying at Perkins all the time. I would come home on weekends. Here is the routine that we established. Every Friday afternoon, a taxi would take me from the campus to the bus station in Boston, where I would board a bus for home. A very nice Upper School boy accompanied me, because he happened to live in the town next to New Bedford. Either my mother or someone else would meet me at the bus terminal every Friday evening. On Sunday afternoons, my father was able to drive me to Perkins, where I usually arrived an hour before supper.

My family and I arrived at the Perkins campus at approximately 4:00 that Sunday afternoon, and suddenly the major adjustment period in my life had begun.

There were two sections of Perkins, the Lower School and the Upper School. Children who attended elementary school stayed in the Lower School, while junior high and high school students stayed in the Upper School. I was to be a Lower School student.

As you walked into the Lower School courtyard, you would see two cottages on your left and two cottages on your right. The first cottage on the left was called Anagnos, named after the founder of the Perkins Kindergarten, Michael Anagnos. Anagnos

Cottage consisted of young boys and girls. Many were in the lower grades, and some had special needs. The next cottage was Potter, the one I would be living in. The boys who lived in Potter were usually in grades four, five, and six, but occasionally a few third–graders were invited if there was room. The first cottage on the right-hand side of the Lower School courtyard was Bradlee, which housed both boys and girls, usually from kindergarten through second grade. The next cottage was Glover, which housed the older girls, grades four through six, but also a few third–graders.

Each cottage had its own porch, which connected the cottage with a schoolhouse. The Anagnos and Bradlee schoolhouses were located south of their cottages, and the Potter and Glover schoolhouses were located north of their cottages. With this particular setup, the children didn't have to walk too far to go to school. Given that boys and girls were in the same classes, many of the Glover girls went to the Potter schoolhouse, while many of the Potter boys went to the Glover schoolhouse. The same applied to the Anagnos and Bradlee schoolhouses.

To put it all in perspective, the entire cottage/schoolhouse combination was all joined together by either a corridor or a porch. This proved to be convenient in bad weather, because none of the kids needed to be exposed to the cold, the rain, or the snow as they traveled to and from school.

The one other feature in the Lower School that I'd like to talk about is the section in the middle of the corridor that separated the Potter schoolhouse from the Glover schoolhouse on the north side of the courtyard. In this section were the gymnasium, the assembly hall, and the library. Upstairs were the science lab and the arts and crafts classroom.

My family stayed with me for a little while in Potter as we all met some of the boys and staff. The main housemother, whom I will call Mrs. Anderson, was a take–charge housemother who was more than happy to show me around different sections of the cottage.

As you walk in the main door of Potter, which is at the porch which connects the cottage to its schoolhouse, there's a locker room. On three walls, there were approximately 35 different lockers, each one with a boy's name on the door. Each boy would keep his coat, sweater, or any other essentials in his locker. In the middle of the locker room was a large bench surrounding a central heating system, and to the left were the bathroom and the door leading upstairs.

If you walked through the locker room, you entered the playroom. In the playroom, there were lots of tables and chairs. Next to the left wall was a huge shuffleboard, and on the right was a big window overlooking the playground. Next to the window was a wall of cubicles where each boy would put his books, because the playroom was used as a study room quite often. Directly ahead, as you walked through the playroom, was a sitting room, and to the right of the sitting room was the main dining room. Potter Cottage, like all the other cottages in the Lower School, had three floors. The second and third floors consisted mainly of bedrooms and a huge bathroom.

After my family said their goodbyes, and after many tears were shed, I was introduced to several of the boys. For now, I will mention four of them who became my friends.

The first boy, Everett, was totally blind. He had lost his sight two years earlier from a brain tumor. Everett had difficulty adjusting, and he possessed lots of fears and insecurities. He didn't go home on the weekends because he lived in Maine. It became apparent that Everett had a very close bond with his mother, and when he was put in a situation he couldn't deal with, he cried out for her. Despite Everett's fragility, he was involved in much of what was going on in the cottage, and I became his friend. Though I didn't have the fears he had, I was very homesick, so I guess our personalities fed off each other, which helped form the friendship.

The second boy was Tony, a sixth-grader from Massachusetts. The thing about Tony that made an impression on everyone was that he was the most active trader in the cottage. It seemed that whenever he was tired of a toy, a radio, or any of a number of other possessions, he would trade them for someone else's.

Albert lived in New Hampshire. He was into science, outer space, and music. He would make up his own adventures and had a vivid imagination. His memory rivaled anyone else's, and I found myself challenging him about when certain events took place in history or in his own personal life. Given that Albert loved talking about the planets in our solar system, I think about him when I remember how scientists removed Pluto as a planet in 2006. Unlike Everett and Tony, Albert had sight, probably as much as I had.

Alex, also from Massachusetts, was another boy with usable vision and a vivid imagination. He used to research scientific facts, and he impressed me with his passion for weather. Being that I was also fascinated by weather, Alex and I talked about it quite often. One thing I recall about him is that he had a talent for knowing the exact temperature outside without finding out about it.

Several of the boys in Potter Cottage were deaf as well as blind, including a victim of the Vietnam War.

There were three housemothers in the cottage, and each had her own unique personality. I had already met Mrs. Anderson, the head housemother, but there were two more housemothers that I had to meet. Miss Tulley was a disciplinarian, but she commanded respect from everyone. To this day, Miss Tulley, who currently lives in Watertown, refers to us as "her boys." She treated each one of us like her own child. She was kind to us if we did well, and took us to task when we made mistakes. In short, she acted like a true mom. I even remember playing checkers with her several times. While Miss Tulley was never married, and probably wanted children of her own, she practiced on us, and she did her job quite well. The third housemother, Miss Jones, was a younger and tougher individual who seemed to act more like one of our peers than our housemother.

In a normal seven–day week, two of the three housemothers were on duty, while the third was off. The housemothers arranged their own schedule, so each would be out on different days.

At 5:30, the boys were called into supper. After supper, we spent time in the Potter playroom until it was time to go upstairs, wash up, and go to bed. For those of us who had our bedrooms on the second floor, bedtime was at 8:00. Third–floor boys went to bed at 8:30. Those were usually the older, sixth-grade boys. As I will refer to later, I was assigned to the fifth-grade class, which meant that the principal had decided to put me back a grade after my evaluation in April. As you recall, I spent my evaluation day in a sixth–grade classroom. I feel that the principal made this decision as a precaution, something which was normal when a new student transferred from another school.

After I got ready for bed, I met my first three roommates. I will call them Willie, Winston, and Jimmy. All three boys were younger than I, probably in third grade. Willie and Winston had a lot of vision, while Jimmy was totally blind. The other three obviously knew each other very well, so I lay in bed and listened to them talk for a while, until one of us fell asleep.

Chapter 3

The School Curriculum

Children at Perkins had a busy day; they didn't have very much time to just think. On school days, we were out of bed by 6:30 in the morning. We would wash up, get dressed, and make our beds. Before we even went downstairs for breakfast, a housemother had to make sure our beds passed inspection. If not, we'd have to do them over again. Breakfast was at 7:30, and many times, study period was at 8:00. The school day began at 9:00, with a 15-minute recess from 10:30 to 10:45. At noon, we broke for lunch, and depending on our afternoon schedule, we returned to school at 1:00, 1:30, or 2:00. It was our job to know our schedules and report to school when the housemother rang the bell. She had to ring it three times because of the three different schedules.

Our school day ended at either 4:00 or 4:30, which didn't give us that much time to play before supper, which was at 5:30 every evening. After supper, we either had study hall or played some more, depending on what the cottage policy makers decided. No matter what we did after supper, we were supervised by young teacher trainees while the housemothers had their supper or a rest period. Then it was bedtime.

It was no surprise that my first week of school was challenging because of all the new experiences I had to encounter all at once. And to make it even more challenging, school was called off on Tuesday afternoon because of the threat of Hurricane Gerda.

On Monday morning at 9:00, I reported to the fifth–grade classroom, which was located in the Potter schoolhouse. I only had to walk approximately 50 feet to school every day. That was pretty neat. Our teacher, Mr. Mack, taught us English, math, and social studies, and occasionally we would have trivia games and write compositions.

On the first day, I learned that Everett and Albert were in my class, and that's when I found out more about Everett's fears and Albert's vivid imagination, because certain situations occurred which brought those characteristics out more. There were three other children in the class. Jane was the only girl. Since she was a resident of Glover Cottage, her walk to school was longer than mine, because the classroom was in the Potter schoolhouse. She was bright, down to earth, and was able to read print text. Jane lived in Massachusetts and had more vision than anyone else in the class.

Quinn was a day student, because he lived very close to the Perkins campus. He was one of the most entertaining kids I met at that time, and he made me laugh during a period in my life when I needed laughter. Quinn could imitate a motorcycle really well. He would run across the room making very realistic motorcycle noises, but at least he had the respect not to do it in front of Mr. Mack. However, Quinn was also a daredevil. One day, we were standing at the top of a stairwell, consisting of 15 stairs to the landing. With one leap, Quinn jumped from the top step onto the landing, feet first.

Besides me, Ike was the only other Perkins newcomer in the fifth–grade class. He lived in Rhode Island, and he had a very jolly personality most of the time, unless he was extremely disappointed about something.

On the first day, I was given my own Braille machine, which I was to take back and forth between the cottage and the classroom. Since many Braille machines were given out, each had its own number, so it could be identified should anything happen to it. The number on my Braille machine was 155. It was not surprising that I had my own Braille machine. For one thing, it was expected, and for another, I had four years of Braille experience at the time.

Though the Braille machine was a very familiar tool, I was soon introduced to a tool I had never used before, one which I found fascinating once I learned how to use it. The device was an abacus. Some of you already know what an abacus is, but for those who don't, I will explain it the best way I can. First of all, I regard the abacus as a very old-fashioned sort of calculator that you operate exclusively by hand. The abacus allows you to add, subtract, multiply, and divide by sliding beads up and down the spindles. The abacus has 13 columns of beads, designed for thirteen decimal places. The style we used included a felt background.

One of the things I admired about Mr. Mack was that he allowed his students to use their imaginations. Once a week, we wrote our own compositions about different topics, and on one or two occasions during the school year, we would participate in a madlib. A madlib is a composition with words missing from it. Without knowing what the composition is about, you're asked to fill in the blank with a noun, verb, adjective, or adverb. Once everyone filled in the missing words with their own, Mr. Mack read the newly formed composition aloud, which made us all laugh.

Our school mornings consisted of studying academic subjects in the home room. Our afternoons, however, were a little different, as we then took courses outside the home room, except for two or three periods per week when we studied a little history, geography, or social studies. This was the case during my fifth- and sixth-grade years, when I had classes in the home room in the morning and courses outside the home room in the afternoon.

On Wednesday mornings at 10:00, the Lower School children gathered in the assembly hall. For half an hour, hymns were sung, followed by a speech from the school director. Then there was a program which consisted of either a guest speaker or a presentation from a Lower School class. When I was in the fifth grade, Mr. Mack's class, together with another class, wrote a play which we all performed during one of the morning assemblies. It was about a boy who was trapped in a library with a variety of books, and he didn't know what to do. Jane introduced the play, Albert played the boy, and the rest of the students were dressed up as books. On another occasion, my class ran a trivia contest in Lower School Assembly, with other classes participating.

Four days a week, Lower School children took singing. Not only did we learn hymns, but we also learned the Perkins Alma Mater, as well as songs for special occasions, such as Christmas concerts, Final Assembly, and the anniversary of the founding of the Perkins Kindergarten. Perkins held three Christmas concerts a year: one for the general public, one for the student body, and one for the parents. We had numerous rehearsals several weeks prior to the concerts. The rehearsals were so frequent that at times they interrupted our school curriculum. The Upper School chorus was involved in the concerts with us.

Another course that we had in fifth grade was sulfeggio. I had never heard that term before we were given our schedules. Sulfeggio is another word for music Braille. We learned how to read musical notes and practiced on different musical instruments. I was introduced to the bongo drums, the resonator bells, the marimba, and the glockenspiel. Some of the boys made fun of the word "sulfeggio." One boy referred to it as liquid detergent.

Once a week, all the lower–school children attended religion class for an hour. Each child was assigned to a particular group based on his or her religious background. I attended Catholic classes, which were taught by a nun.

In crafts, I remember making several change purses, a top, and an item made from liquid plaster.

For one hour a week, we had science, which was one of my favorite subjects outside the homeroom, our main classroom. Among some of the topics we covered were motion, water and air temperature, chemical reactions, electricity, and the career of Harvey, the white rabbit that our teacher kept in the lab. During my first year in science class, we discovered that it took nine D–cell batteries in a circuit to burn out a flashlight bulb, and as many as 39 D–cell batteries to make a regular light bulb glow dimly.

However, the most fascinating and noteworthy science project in my entire two years of Lower School was the creation of an erupting volcano. Once we finished it and knew that it worked, we were so proud of our accomplishment that we decided to give the volcano a name. Well, it just so happened that at the same time we made the volcano, our class was studying the eruption of Mt. Vesuvius, the one that destroyed the Roman city of Pompeii in AD 79. Being that it was a Lower School project, the class agreed to name our volcano Lower Skoovius. From what I understand, Lower Skoovius was given to the Perkins museum for display.

In gym class, we learned everything from doing forward rolls to climbing rope ladders. This was a class where Everett's fears became quite obvious. It seemed to me that with the loss of his sight, he had become so out of touch with his surroundings that he couldn't trust his own body. Admittedly, I had a fear of heights, too, so that when we climbed rope ladders, I was more than a bit apprehensive.

However, in Everett's case, he was not only afraid of heights, but he was also afraid to do a forward roll. At one point, the gym teacher made him do the forward roll by pushing his body into it, which didn't solve the problem where Everett was concerned. Sometimes, though, gym was fun. We did some running, sit-ups, push-ups, jumping jacks, squat thrusts, and other exercises to warm up all of our muscles. The biggest mistake I always seemed to make when doing push-ups was to touch the floor with my knees. I learned very quickly that this is not an effective way to do a push-up. Your legs have to be straight at all times, while you use your arms to lift and lower your body.

In the Lower School, we were required to take swimming. In my first year, the boys and girls took swimming separately, so we were allowed to go into the pool without bathing suits on. However, when the boys and girls swam together the following year, bathing suits were required.

Once a week, the children had an opportunity to shop at the Perkins store, which was set up in the Lower School principal's office. Most of the merchandise consisted of objects that cost a nickel or a dime. They included small toy musical instruments, toy cars, and other odds and ends.

Chapter 4

Things that Make You Go "Hmmm"

For reasons that I still don't quite understand, I developed a reputation during my first few weeks at Perkins which I found extremely annoying. That is, it was believed that I had a lot more vision than I was actually using. If I hadn't been so shy and so intimidated, or if I hadn't had complete respect for my housemothers no matter how they behaved, I would have asked the obvious question. The housemothers knew how extremely upset and emotional I was on my first day away from home. Knowing this fact, why would they believe that I'd want to leave my parents and go to a school for the blind 65 miles away from home in order to pretend not to have all of my sight? Wouldn't I simply have stayed in the New Bedford school system? Nonetheless, Miss Tulley and Miss Jones didn't recognize the logic of this, and they proceeded to make a jackass of me about my vision – that is, until my mother finally made a trip to the school to shut them up.

I had been at the school for only two or three days before Miss Tulley decided I was faking. She knew that I had usable vision, but she felt I didn't use enough of it. So here's what she did.

In the large bathroom on the second floor of Potter Cottage, each of the boys had his own towel and face cloth on a hook. Behind each hook was the boy's name, written in indelible pencil on a piece of long adhesive tape attached to the wall. I was not concerned with whether each boy could see his own name. After all, I was in a school for the blind, and although some boys had more vision than others, I assumed that the indelible names were there for the benefit of the staff, in case a boy questioned where his towel and face cloth were.

Miss Tulley obviously had her own agenda and decided to single me out. Before we all washed up for bed one evening, she took me into a room, which I presumed was her office. She gave me a large piece of paper and a magic marker and asked me to write my name in big bold letters, so that I could prove to her that I could find my towel and face cloth by looking for my name.

Once the large piece of paper with my name appeared on the wall amidst all the other boys' names on strips of adhesive tape, Miss Tulley asked me to walk into the bathroom and locate my name. I remember having a hard time locating my name. I don't know. Perhaps the lighting in the bathroom wasn't the best, or maybe the color of the paper blended in with the tiles on the wall, or perhaps I simply didn't have enough distance vision to be able to do that. All I know is that Miss Tulley wasn't satisfied, so she asked me to do it again. By this time, I was extremely irritated with her. Why was I the only boy in the entire cottage receiving this treatment? To this very day, I still don't have the answer.

Eventually, Miss Tulley stopped putting me through the horrors of walking back and forth from her office to the bathroom, but she wasn't done with me yet. When I was finished washing up, I went into the bedroom which I shared with Willie, Winston, and Jimmy. To my surprise, as I walked into the room, the boys who were there told me that it was the wrong one. But how could it be the wrong room? I had spent the first few nights in that room, and I knew exactly where it was and whom I roomed with. It seemed that my bedroom had been switched on me behind my back, and Miss Tulley wanted me to find it on my own. According to her, given that I supposedly had the vision of Superman, I should have been able to see my name on a door.

Finally, and for whatever reason, Miss Tulley gave up, and I was introduced to my new bedroom and roommates. I've often been asked if my three original roommates were in on the plot. I don't think so. It may be that the boys believed I had been told about the switch in bedrooms, and that I had simply forgotten about it when I poked my head in the door.

However, this was not the end of the abuse that I took in connection with the housemothers' opinions about my vision. One morning after breakfast, when I thought I was going to enjoy some playtime before school, one of the housemothers, who I believe was Miss Jones, decided to take me out to the playground herself. Oh, but there wasn't going to be any playtime! Miss Jones brought me from boy to boy, asking me to identify the color of something he was wearing. Who was she kidding? This was a school for the blind! Miss Jones, like any other staff member, was hired to care for blind children. If I had needed to try to identify colors, that's a test that should have been done in a doctor's office.

Can you imagine how I felt that morning? While all the other boys were swinging on the swings, riding the seesaw, playing ball, using the jungle gym, or playing hide and seek, I was being asked, "What color is Tommy's coat? What color are Joey's pants? What color is Johnny's shirt?" I guarantee you that no other student was ever treated in this fashion, or I would have heard about that by now. As recently as this year, a friend of mine who was in Potter with me at the time told me that he remembers the incident well, and he thought that Miss Jones was absolutely cruel. However, as I stated earlier, we were, to some extent, intimidated, and my long-time friend agrees with me on that to this day. I firmly believe that Miss Jones and Miss Tulley would be in court today if the two incidents I just described, as well as several other incidents, had happened in 2012 instead of in 1969. There is no doubt in my mind about that.

Yes, there were other incidents in the cottage besides the ones I just told you about.

It's one thing for a housemother to be concerned when a child isn't eating properly, but it's another thing if she takes her concern to a new level, one that borders on abuse. One morning during breakfast, I wasn't eating all of my cereal. I don't remember why that was the case, nor do I think it matters. The point is that I wasn't allowed to leave the dining room and go about my day unless I finished my cereal. It didn't matter that I had to get ready for school. I had to finish the cereal or I wasn't going anywhere.

I remember the housemothers leaving the dining room, where I was placed under the supervision of the kitchen help. The Scottish woman in charge of the kitchen reinforced what the housemothers said. If I didn't eat my cereal, I would be sitting in my chair for a long, long time. At 12 years old, I was probably too young to define a conspiracy, but in the back of my mind, I felt there was a conspiracy against me for sure.

I don't remember how it happened, but finally, I was allowed to go to school without finishing my cereal. I was so glad that my ordeal was over. But was it?

After I spent the morning in school, I went back to Potter Cottage for lunch. There, I was completely overwhelmed by the smell of fried chicken. It reminded me of my mom's home cooking. I proudly walked into the dining room with everyone else, sat in my chair, and anxiously waited for my fried chicken while my mouth watered. Well, as it turned out, my hopes of having fried chicken were destroyed when I discovered that my bowl of unfinished cereal was still at my place setting. If I had been as vocal as I am today, I would have had many choice words for those housemothers.

Not only did the other boys and staff eat lunch in the dining room, but several teachers also spent their lunch hour in the cottages instead of going home. On this particular day, they were all enjoying fried chicken. Yet there I sat, with the unfinished bowl of cereal in front of me, while a teacher at my table told me to finish it before I could have any chicken. She wasn't even my teacher or my housemother. So was I suddenly the focal point of the whole unpleasant situation? The star of the show? The center of all the negative attention in the world? Perhaps it was no wonder that I went home every weekend crying to my parents about how I couldn't tolerate living at Perkins.

In all honesty, I don't remember if I had a piece of chicken that day or not, but I do remember how shabbily I was being treated. Some may say that the housemothers' intentions were good. It's okay to care about a child and to make sure that he eats what he's supposed to eat. However, I feel that there is a point where you have to sit down and decide how to handle a situation like this without stepping outside the box, outside the bounds of common sense.

If you think that the incident with the cereal was bad enough, believe me, it got worse.

One Thursday evening, we were all in the dining room having our supper. Toward the end of the meal, when it became apparent that some of us weren't finishing our food, we were given some very unpleasant news. I believe that the news was delivered to us by a housemother, and if not, the housemother, by her own actions, supported and endorsed it.

We were told that tonight was to be Execution Night, an annual Perkins event which took place in order to punish a student who ate the least amount of food. To make the point even further, I was given an example of what supposedly happened to a girl on Execution Night the year before. Allegedly, she had her arm broken. With all the negative treatment I had already received that September, I had sort of become immune to more bad news and took their word for it. So I tried to eat as much as I could while imagining myself being escorted to the jungle gym for execution. Of course, there was no execution.

One night, after the housemothers had decided that I was going to eat like a bird at every meal, they did the following, believing I'd have no problem with it since I was a picky eater. We had hamburgers for supper, one of my favorite foods. I knew I would eat the entire hamburger, but the housemother thought not. She served me a small piece, probably one eighth the size of the entire burger. Her attitude was, since I had trouble eating other foods, she was going to start me out with a very tiny piece of the burger, and if I ate it, she'd give me another tiny piece. Now, I don't want you to think that this behavior by the housemothers happened every day. Far from it. However, when they were in the mood to try to prove their own warped version of some point, they did.

In Chapter 2, I described Miss Jones as a younger and tougher housemother, who at times acted like she was one of our peers. I realize that taking care of 35 boys is a major responsibility, but if you can't handle it, you shouldn't be in the profession. My friend Everett was a diabetic. I say "was" because he passed away several years ago in Maine. One night, Miss Jones decided to give Everett an insulin shot during supper. Like other boys his age, Everett dreaded the needle. I know that anybody can tell a little boy to "get over it," but I believe that telling a boy to simply get over it doesn't solve the problem. The boy has to motivate himself to be tough enough to take the shot. I didn't hear much of the conversation between Everett and Miss Jones about the shot he was about to have, but knowing Miss Jones' personality, I assume she told Everett to get over it.

Suddenly, I heard Everett cry out loud. I understood why. As I explained early in my description of Everett, something serious happened to his confidence when he lost his sight. After Everett began to cry, and when he expressed his desire not to take his insulin shot, Miss Jones proceeded to get everyone's attention. She then announced that we had a big baby in the dining room, and that his name was Everett. I don't know how embarrassed Everett felt about that, but I know that I was embarrassed for him.

In my sixth-grade year, Miss Jones was replaced by the Scottish woman who used to be in charge of the kitchen, Miss Carma. Miss Jones needed to be replaced, but if they were going to replace her, it should have been with someone better. Miss Carma had similar character flaws and was abusive. One day, she grabbed me very hard by the arm. I showed the mark to my mother, who then ratted Miss Carma out to the head housemother. Miss Carma apologized.

With that said, I can't stand it when a bully uses a child's weakness and twists it around to his or her advantage in order to get another child to do something that he doesn't want to. For example, Miss Carma wanted me to slide down a ramp on the playground one day, and I refused to do it. The way she tried to convince me to do it was by insisting that Everett had tried it and had loved every second of it. I knew Everett very well, so I didn't believe that about him. I had spent many hours with him in gym class and knew that he was a very frightened boy. I could just picture Miss Carma pushing Everett down the ramp while he screamed at the top of his lungs, so she shouldn't have tried to talk me into sliding down the ramp by lying about Everett.

In the Lower School, as part of our school curriculum, groups of boys got together once a week for group guidance. Yes, there was private guidance and there was group guidance. Private guidance was a session between a child and his counselor, where the child felt free to talk about whatever he wanted. Group guidance was designed to improve group interaction, but it became a gossip session. Boys in the group would talk about other children who weren't there to defend themselves, and the teacher didn't stop it.

I remember hearing in the group that an Upper School girl was terrified that she might be pregnant because she had kissed a boy. I don't believe the girl would have appreciated being talked about in a professional group setting. Obviously, kids get together all the time and talk about people. That's normal. But in my opinion, to use a professional environment as a forum for discussing a 15–year–old girl's fear of being pregnant based on a kiss was more than questionable. The girl may have had psychological problems, or perhaps she had been so sheltered that she assumed you can become pregnant from a kiss. In any case, talking about this during a group guidance session was entirely inappropriate.

Chapter 5

Fun and Fury

During my two years in the Lower School, I also had a lot of good times, both in the school setting and with my friends in the cottage. Finally, the ridiculous abuse by one or more of the housemothers seemed to have come to an end, though the strict disciplinary attitude of Miss Tulley remained, which was a good thing. Miss Jones continued to display her bullying personality, as did Miss Carma, her successor. However, I figured out a way to rise above all that, despite my shyness.

I played shuffleboard and checkers with many of the boys in the cottage, but when we were out on the playground, I bowled, played baseball, and participated in a fascinating game called Red Rover. I described the outdoor bowling alley when I talked about my evaluation day at Perkins. As for baseball, we were taught to wait for the ball to bounce in front of home plate before we swung the bat. I wasn't one of the best players in Potter, or in any other cottage later on, but I always had fun participating.

In the spring of 1971, toward the end of my sixth–grade year, the gym teacher formed a small baseball league within Potter. There were certainly enough boys in the cottage, so four teams were formed: the gold team, the green team, the purple team, and the blue team. We played ball for approximately three weeks as the teams competed against each other for the championship. Red Rover was a game I had never heard of until I was at Perkins. Several boys would form a circle. The object of the game was to send one of the boys to the other side of the circle where he would try to break out. Also, for those boys who wanted to test their basketball shooting abilities, there was a basketball hoop on the outside wall of Potter Cottage, facing the playground.

When the boys weren't playing games or simply having fun on the playground or in the cottage, there was study time. At times, study period took place after supper or after breakfast, and it normally lasted for a half hour. This gave us a chance to do our homework without being disturbed. For the most part, study periods were very routine. The boys were quiet, and all you heard were the clicking of Braille writers. Remember that some of the boys had enough sight to read print, while others needed Braille.

One evening, Miss Jones tried to show her true colors again. But this time, it was my buddy Alex who had the last laugh, even though a lot of unnecessary embarrassment was caused in the process. And I wouldn't wish what happened to Alex on anybody.

Alex politely got up from his chair and asked Miss Jones if he could be excused for a minute. When Miss Jones sharply said no, Alex proceeded to vomit all over the floor. There are several ways to look at this situation. Would Miss Jones have let Alex go to the bathroom if he had asked to go? All he asked was if he could be excused for a minute. Also, Miss Jones could have asked Alex why he needed to be excused, but she didn't. Nonetheless, this incident reinforced my belief that whenever a student in a classroom or a study hall or any other formal setting needs to leave for any reason, you should let him leave. If he's a questionable kid, then follow him or have a professional official on hand to monitor him if he tries anything foolish.

After Alex vomited all over the floor, the only thing I could think of was how, despite his embarrassment and his being sick, he had the last laugh. And given all the bullying behavior that Miss Jones had already demonstrated in the cottage, I was not on her side at all.

During another study period after breakfast one morning, there was more drama. At that time, Miss Carma, the other bully, was in charge of the kitchen and not yet a housemother. At the same time, there was a new boy, Carlos, who had come to Perkins in the middle of the school year. I don't know how it started, but suddenly Carlos and Miss Carma were in a physical fight in the locker room where we kept our coats. We could all hear the lockers as the two banged against them: *Boom, boom, boom!* The fight went on for approximately two minutes, and to this day, I don't know what it was all about.

Aside from the housemothers, we had housemasters and teacher trainees looking after us. The housemasters were available during some of the play time, and they occasionally became involved in off–campus activities for the boys. The trainees supervised us while the housemothers ate their meals or were in a private meeting. Many of us developed a special attachment to the teacher trainees, because they were a lot younger than most of the housemothers, and they acted more like our peers than our superiors.

One day, Mrs. Anderson, the head housemother, had what she thought was a great idea, though I disagreed with it intensely. Each staff member was asked to vote for her favorite Potter boy. The boy with the most votes would receive a special gift. Some of you may find nothing wrong with this, but if you really think about it, this was a potentially dangerous project. Keep in mind the sensitivity, age, and self–esteem of some of the boys. They may have regarded this as a form of favoritism, potentially causing resentment toward a particular staff member or among the boys themselves. If you were a boy in my cottage, and you found out that a teacher trainee had voted for me as her favorite boy, how would you feel? It's true that the staff could have been asked to keep their votes a secret, but that's never a sure thing, as you know.

While I was in Lower School, I joined the Boy Scouts. Both of our housemasters, Mr. Andre and Mr. Martin, were two of the troop leaders, along with Mr. Gray, an Upper School work activities teacher. I was not in Boy Scouts for very long, but during my time in the program, I learned a few things. I learned how to tie different kinds of knots, I paddled on the Perkins pond in a canoe, and I learned how to trust myself a little more.

The Boy Scouts were divided into smaller groups called patrols. Each patrol had a president, a vice–president, and a scribe. I believe a scribe is similar to a clerk or secretary. The Boy Scouts weren't always doing serious projects; we had fun as well. During one of our sessions, we went to the gym and played a game called Steal the Bacon. This game was similar to tug–of–war, only we used our feet to control a flat object that looked like a large strip of bacon.

On a given day each May, the kids at Perkins were treated to another exciting annual outdoor spring event, known as Kite Day. Prizes were given to those who held the distinction of having the kite that spent the most time in the air, or the highest flying kite. I suppose this was the only occasion where the faculty could actually get away with telling us to go fly a kite and mean it.

I've talked about a lot of what we did in our spare time, but I can't finish this chapter without talking about girls. Although Perkins had very strict rules at the time about how the boys and girls should or shouldn't interact, we did spend time with them in class, and we got to know them pretty well. However, after school, the boys and girls went their separate ways, meaning the end of interaction between the sexes until the next day.

Though we accepted the routine, that didn't stop some of us from developing crushes on particular girls. I remember liking a girl who was one grade ahead of me, but I was too shy to express it. Then again, even though I was shy, the rules about male and female interaction also prevented a lot of us from acting out our feelings. How could we spend quality time with the girls? Should we dance in the science lab, or kiss in the middle of math? Keep in mind that we're not talking about children who were eight or nine years old. We're talking about 11-, 12-, and 13-year-olds.

Perkins was so firm with its rules about dating on campus that when they eventually tried to become a bit more progressive, it was a shock. I remember the day that the announcement ripped through Potter Cottage loud and clear. There was going to be a supper exchange! Half the boys would eat with half the girls, and the other half of the girls would eat with the other half of the boys. Needless to say, children who go to school in their home town would think nothing of this. However, at Perkins, this was a big, big deal at the time!

I also remember wrestling with a couple of boys on the grass on the Potter playground. The purpose was to find out who would win a certain girl that we all liked. I lost these wrestling matches, but the boys involved became very good friends of mine.

In November of 1969, the boys and girls got together in the gym for a unique event called "The Happening." It was not regular gym, just a social gathering during school time. It took place at 1:00 in the afternoon, before the afternoon school session, and it included games, good music, and a blanket toss. During the blanket toss, you would place yourself on the blanket while the teachers lifted it up off the ground. The object of the blanket toss was to get you to bounce up from the blanket while the teachers moved it up and down as if they were airing it out.

It seemed as if the teachers who participated in the activities at The Happening had as good a time as the kids. I suppose it was their way of reliving their youth all over again. However, The Happening was a one-time event.

Though I had sex education on two different occasions in the Upper School, and though my mother believed that I hadn't learned the facts of life until I was at least 16, I actually learned a distorted version of the birds and the bees at age 12 from several of the boys in my cottage who talked about sex and told dirty jokes. We all know that 10-year-olds are quite capable of discussing sex and telling dirty jokes, but I feel that my mom would have been shocked if she had heard some of the language coming from the mouths of these boys at ages 10 and 11.

Chapter 6

Religion, Health, Safety, and Adventure

As I pointed out earlier, religion played a role in the Perkins scheme of things. When I was in fifth grade, the entire student body had religion class once a week, usually on Thursdays from 3:00 to 4:00 p.m. Though most of us are churchgoers and have faith in God, there are a lot of people who continue to ask questions. In my religion class, it was very refreshing to hear the children ask questions, because that showed an interest in the subject matter. In my opinion as a Catholic, God would much rather we inquire about him than not pay attention.

Aside from religion classes, the administration at Perkins did their best to make sure we celebrated holy days of obligation. I remember waking up very early on several occasions to attend Catholic Mass on Ascension Day and on another occasion in the fall. I can't speak for the other religions, but on the Catholic holy days of obligation during the week, a bus would pick us up and bring us to and from the Catholic church in Watertown before our school day began. Though I did not stay at Perkins on weekends, it is my understanding that the children who wanted to go to church off campus had the necessary transportation.

While Perkins tried to consider all religions on many levels, the school took a bit of heat at times. Each year, Jewish students were allowed to miss school during Rosh Hashanah and Yom Kippur while the rest of us had to attend class on those days. I thought that was a nice gesture on Perkins' part, and I respected the decision. Despite how I felt, some of the children were jealous that they had to go to school during the Jewish holidays. However, the counterargument was that Jewish students didn't take time off during Hanukkah unless it conflicted with Christmas. Also, they participated in all of the Christmas activities Perkins had to offer. As for the Catholics, we always took Christmas off, but I recall several times when we actually went to school at least half the day on Good Friday. When you look at the whole picture, the religious privileges were distributed as fairly as Perkins could have done it, but as you know, no matter how fair something is, someone is always going to question it.

If any of us were ill or needed a checkup, we went to a small infirmary on the campus. Perkins had its own doctor, nurse, and dentist. I remember that during my third day of school, as I was walking across the Lower School courtyard to get to class, I felt something prick my thumb. I thought I was stung, so I made my concerns known and went to the infirmary. The staff proceeded to put alcohol on the affected area, and then I went back to school. To this day, I'm still wondering whether it was a bee sting or prickly cactus.

Perkins cared a lot about the major diseases that affected people in the old days, and did its best to monitor the children in that way. On several occasions during my time in the Lower School, the children were all sent to the infirmary to be tested for tuberculosis. The test required two visits to the infirmary in a given week. On the first day, we were each given an injection of a substance called tuberculin on the inside of the forearm, just under the skin. Two days later we were asked to return to have the area on the arm evaluated. How the skin reacted determined whether we had tuberculosis. The test was known as the Mantoux test.

During my stay at Perkins, the first thing I thought of when spending time with the other children was that they all had issues with their vision. After all, this is a school for the blind, so I felt that blindness was the main focal point in these kids' lives. It occurred to me that many of these children had other health problems, but I didn't realize at first how serious some of their problems actually were. Several of these kids died during their stay at Perkins, and it was then that the reality hit me. I believe that the most common cause of death among the children who died while at Perkins was a brain tumor. Many had diabetes, but of those who died from it eventually, most had survived until quite recently.

Until I went to Perkins, I had never witnessed an epileptic seizure. I didn't know what one was, or how it was handled, until one day in religion class. One of my classmates who lived in Anagnos Cottage has a learning disability, yet that didn't stop him from asking all the right questions of the Sister.

One day, the boy fell off his chair and onto the floor. You can imagine the panic in the class as a result. In the back of our minds, we thought something very serious had happened to the boy. When the Sister lifted him up off the floor, expressing her concern for his health, the boy insisted that he was fine. Later, I learned that he had had an epileptic seizure, and I assumed that it wasn't his first, because of how he reacted to it.

I knew another boy from Anagnos Cottage who wore a helmet all the time in case he hit his head during his seizures. Another boy who lived in Potter during my sixth-grade year was extremely tall and lanky for 10 years old. He had a poor appetite, and the housemothers used to get on his case for not eating. Later it was learned that the boy died from a rare disease which I can't describe, just that his bone structure allowed him to be nearly six feet tall and weigh only 60 pounds.

The Perkins faculty and administration also cared a great deal about our safety. Everyone should learn what to do in case of a fire, and Perkins taught us well. Several times a year, we had surprise fire drills. If we were in a Lower School class, our job was to report to our cottages and wait for the all–clear signal to sound. During my fifth–grade year, the fire alarm was simply the repeated ringing of the school bell, the same school bell that sounded between classes. Before I was a student at Perkins, the children used to undergo shelter drills, especially during the time of the Cuban Missile Crisis. Perkins had a lot of tunnels under the campus, and below one of the tunnels was a bomb shelter, which was available in case we needed it.

With all that I said about the ringing of the school bell as a fire alarm, steps were being taken to upgrade that situation. One evening in October 1969, we were playing in the Potter playground as we normally did, when suddenly we heard an unfamiliar buzzing sound in the distance. We all wondered what it was, but it didn't take long to figure it out. We were summoned into Potter Cottage, where the source of the buzzing sound was. Needless to say, it was a very loud sound, and it was long and steady for a few minutes. When the noise stopped, and when we were able to converse again, we were told what had happened. Based on the information I received, I concluded that Perkins had installed a brand–new fire alarm, and that it was being tested. Later I learned that the alarm had been pulled by one of the Potter boys, the deaf–blind boy from Vietnam.

For those people in society who believe that the blind can't compete on equal terms with the sighted, we explain how we can, given the proper training. We can compete for jobs, live independent lives, and pull fire alarms just like the sighted can. The new fire alarm system was not used during my fifth–grade year for actual fire drills, though we all knew it worked in Potter. It wasn't until the fall of 1970 that the new alarm was sounded in a fire drill.

Though I believe Perkins did what it could to keep us safe, I think they blew it on October 23, 1970. It was 1:00 in the afternoon, and we were in our sixth-grade classroom in the Glover schoolhouse. Suddenly there was a fire drill, and we went back to our cottages as we normally did. As we sat in Potter Cottage waiting for the all-clear signal, it became apparent that this was not a traditional fire drill. I heard staff walking around the cottage, making and waiting for phone calls. Finally, we learned that someone had called in a bomb threat, and that we should leave our cottage, go to the Upper School, and report to Dwight Hall, the auditorium in the main building where concerts were held.

During the bomb scare, it didn't occur to me what was wrong with this logic. I made my way to Dwight Hall with the boys and the Potter staff. When I arrived, I noticed that the entire student body had congregated in the middle of the auditorium. We all stood there, waiting for someone to tell us there was no bomb. Looking back on the situation, I believe Perkins made a huge blunder. Ask yourselves this question: If you ran a private school, and you knew that someone had called in a bomb threat but hadn't told you where the bomb was, would you have the entire student body meet in the middle of the large concert hall in the main building of the entire campus? Being that no one knew where the bomb was, or if there was one at all, didn't it occur to anybody that the bomb might have been planted backstage? Finally, the announcement came that we were free to go. I only learned recently from an old friend that the bomb scare was called in by a Perkins 11th-grader, who ended up dying of leukemia in 1975.

As I mentioned earlier, I used to take the bus home on Friday nights, while accompanied by an older boy from the Upper School who was traveling in the same direction. After a while, I found a more convenient way to go home on weekends.

My father provided some of the transportation when he could, and soon I learned that another boy lived in New Bedford. Arrangements were made for his parents to bring me back home on Fridays with their son. The boy, Rob, was a jolly lad who made his parents proud. I was extremely grateful for the rides, because it was a lot easier than taking cabs, waiting in bus stations, and riding through rush–hour traffic on the expressway.

On April 8, 1971, I experienced one of the most embarrassing moments of my life. It was 12:00 noon on that Thursday, the beginning of a long Easter weekend. My father picked me up to bring me back home. Usually when he came, we made sure everything was packed, because like me, my father, God rest his soul, was an extremely meticulous man. In fact, as we were leaving Potter Cottage for his car, my father asked me one more time if I had forgotten anything, and I insisted I hadn't.

He drove me home and proceeded to go about his day. Moments after I arrived home and greeted my mother for the first time in four days, my mother received a rather disturbing telephone call. It was one of Rob's parents, asking where Rob was. My mother didn't know, so she asked me. I had no clue either, but apparently my father was to give Rob a ride back to New Bedford, because Rob's parents weren't able to do it. I was supposed to get the information and pass it along to my father, but I had never received that message. So Rob's parents had to drive back to Perkins later that day to get their son. I don't know where the source of the communication breakdown was, but I was extremely embarrassed, and sorry for the disruption this caused Rob and his family.

As elementary school children, we were very busy. We got out of bed early, had breakfast, spent hours in school, had supper, and did our homework during study period. Sometimes we were asked to be on dish crew after a meal. During dish crew, it was our job to stack the silverware and dishes, bring them into the kitchen, and wash them. To make our job a little easier, there was a powerful automatic dishwasher. The dish crew consisted of three or four boys, who were selected as part of a rotation process.

When you look at the broader picture, you can see that we didn't have much time for ourselves. However, when we had that time to do as we pleased, we took full advantage of the opportunities we had. I usually spent my free time on the swings, bowling, talking with my friends on the bench, listening to the radio, or playing games in the cottage. On special occasions, the boys participated in activities that were appropriate to the occasion. I remember celebrating Halloween by bobbing for apples, going on treasure hunts, and scaring each other. We had our own Christmas parties in the cottage, and of course there was the Open House luncheon which took place before the children demonstrated their skills to the public. Open House normally took place on a Sunday, either in late March or some time in April. During the last week of school, the boys in Potter spent an entire day at Singing Beach in Manchester, Massachusetts. I had the pleasure of going twice, at the end of my fifth- and sixth-grade years, and I had a lot of fun walking on the sand, jumping waves in the shallow part of the ocean, and eating delicious picnic food.

My parents, though they were separated and generally did not communicate with one another, nonetheless managed to attend many of the Perkins events they were invited to, because they put my interests before their own problems. From my first day at Perkins until the day I graduated, my parents, despite their personal problems, communicated when they had to. Transportation was one of the biggest issues, and usually the issues were resolved.

In the spring of 1970, our New Bedford newspaper learned that I attended Perkins and decided to do a feature story on me. I guess the paper felt I would make quite a human interest story.

Imagine how the readers would react if they read about a blind boy doing his schoolwork, tying his shoes, cutting his meat, and walking around the courtyard with a friend. Have you ever seen human interest stories about sighted children who could do those things?

I honestly don't know how the newspaper found out about me, but one morning while I was in class, a newspaper reporter stopped in. He took pictures of the classroom and of me doing my schoolwork. I went back to Potter, where additional pictures were taken of the courtyard, and of me tying my shoes and having lunch. At one point, they summoned another boy, Doug, to be included in some of the pictures, probably to show the public that I had made a few friends.

Though I get why the newspaper wanted to include pictures of me eating in the dining room and tying my shoes, there are many people today, including activists, who would say that this was an act of exploitation on the part of the newspaper. In other words, what's the big deal about a blind boy tying his shoes, cutting his meat, or reading a book? Though it's not really a big deal, sometimes the public needs to be introduced to the concept, either through stories like these or other examples, such as Open House. In those days, it didn't occur to me that we, the blind children of Perkins, had to prove how self–sufficient we could be. But today, as adults, we need to prove it every day in order to find a job, run a household, or do anything else that sighted people do.

When we were kids, not only did we learn our skills and think nothing of it, but some of the blind children I spent time with went beyond their expected abilities. I've already talked about how my friend Quinn jumped 15 stairs at a time and landed on his feet without a scratch. Other boys learned how to short–sheet beds just to annoy kids they didn't like. The deaf–blind boy from Vietnam put a piece of used chewing gum in my hair one day, and Mrs. Anderson and Miss Jones spent a few frustrating minutes trying to clean out the area with alcohol. While two boys were pulling the fire alarm, another learned how to urinate in a wall socket. Trust me, it wasn't an accident. The lad wanted to find out what the experience felt like.

Earlier, I talked about some of the equipment on the Potter playground. One form of amusement was the giant swing. This particular swing consisted of a long piece of heavy wood, approximately eight feet in length and wide enough for a young child to straddle it. While you are straddling the swing, you are swinging back and forth, but to the observer, the swing is moving sideways. On each end of the wood was a chain which helped suspend it, similar to how traditional baby swings are suspended. Many boys would sit on the giant swing at once. Together, they pushed the long piece of wood into motion, and occasionally pumped it up just to find out how high it would go. One day, several of the more daring boys stood up on the giant swing and held onto the chain while it was swinging over the maximum safe height. At that point, one boy jumped off and landed on the grass eight feet below. The boy escaped without injury, but Miss Tulley, the housemother, though relieved, kindly recommended that he not do it again.

Chapter 7

The Trip to Cape Cod

My second year in the Lower School wasn't much different from the first, at least through February. The routine in Potter Cottage was practically the same, even though Mrs. Anderson and Miss Jones were replaced by two new housemothers. I already told you a little about the behavior of Miss Carma, so I won't be repetitious. The new head housemother, Mrs. Murphy, was a softspoken, motherly lady who very seldom practiced discipline. I believe that the boys respected her so much that discipline wasn't necessary. The two housemasters, Mr. Andre and Mr. Martin, were replaced by Mr. Allison and Mr. Casper.

When I still went to bed on the second floor, my bedtime was still 8:00 p.m., but toward the end of the school year, I was finally transferred to the third floor, where I was awarded an extra half hour before bed. At that point in my life, I felt honored to be a member of the "Third Floor Boys," given the extra privilege I was granted.

The school curriculum was similar. Being that I was now in the sixth grade, I no longer had Mr. Mack for a teacher. Quinn, the boy who leaped down a flight of stairs and imitated the sounds of motorcycles, left Perkins and returned home to his native state of West Virginia. The reason why Quinn was a day student in my fifth-grade year was because he had other relatives close by. Ike stayed back in the fifth grade. However, Everett, Albert, and Jane were promoted with me. In the sixth grade, Jane no longer had to feel weird about being the only girl in the class. Trish, a sixth-grader from the year before, stayed back, while a new girl arrived on the scene, Sandra. Liz, a deaf-blind girl who arrived in the middle of my fifth-grade year, was also part of our new class.

In sixth grade, I learned how to play the piano. The instructor taught me how to read musical notes in Braille and play simple songs. It was the first time in my life that I had formally learned to play a musical instrument. I learned how to jump off the diving board into the deep end of the swimming pool, as did many of the other children. I never thought I would be so motivated, because I was always gun shy of the deep water, but Mr. Joe, my swimming instructor, had a way of motivating his students.

The decision to allow boys and girls to swim together was the first of many changes involving male and female interaction. The separation of boys and girls outside of class was such a tradition at Perkins, that when a decision of any kind was made to bring the opposite sexes together, it was met with quite a reaction. First there was the supper exchange, then a supervised dance in the Lower School gym, then an hour of games between Glover and Potter Cottages in that same gym, and then mixed swimming.

Later in my sixth-grade year, another major decision was made involving relationships between the sexes. For the first time, the principal decided to allow boys and girls to play together on the Potter and Glover playgrounds during morning recess. I thought it was fine, as did most of the other children involved. However, the decision to bring both sexes together during recess wasn't met with full support. One morning, when a girl wanted to use the giant swing in the Potter playground, the boy who was sitting on it had other ideas. First, he expressed his resentment of a girl coming onto his territory. The girl, who was extremely fearless, reminded him of the principal's new rule, but he wouldn't have any of that. He started to pick a fight with her, and the two children became physical. I don't know the end result, but I doubt that the incident had any effect on the principal's original decision to bring both sexes together during recess.

In late February of 1971, more than halfway through my sixth-grade year, some new things began to happen which affected part of what Mr. Mills had to teach us. I didn't know what the purpose of these new occurrences was until much later. Five of the Lower School classes were about to launch a brand-new project that had never been done before. These five classes, including mine, were preparing to spend one week at the Cape Cod National Seashore during the first week of May. So, two months before then, Mr. Mills and the four other teachers began to prepare the children for independent life.

During this time, a new building opened on the Perkins School campus called the North Building, probably named for its location in relation to all the other buildings. On three occasions before the Cape Cod trip, Mr. Mills took our class to the North Building for lunch, so that he could teach us how to make our own meals. The plan for the five classes was very organized. Once we were on Cape Cod, each class, supervised by their own teacher, would rotate between meal prep and clean-up for the five days we'd spend there. During our cooking lessons at the North Building, we were taught how to make such things as French toast, chocolate chip cookies, and invisible hot dogs.

Why did I call them invisible hot dogs? Allow me to explain. When we were planning our hot dog lunch, Mr. Mills wanted the entire class to agree that all of our hot dogs would have the same condiments on them, and if one student disagreed, we'd be eating toasted buns without the hot dogs in them. I don't know why Mr. Mills wouldn't allow us the independence of deciding what we wanted on each hot dog. After all, the trip to Cape Cod was all about independence, among other things, so why couldn't we have the right to pick and choose what we wanted as individual human beings? When asked what we wanted on our hot dogs, everyone agreed to have a plain hot dog except Liz. She wanted ketchup. As a result of Liz being different from the rest of us, we had no hot dogs. Instead of the class telling Mr. Mills how foolish he was being, we allowed ourselves to submit to it. Jane practically begged Liz to have a plain hot dog if we were going to eat any at all, but Liz, who showed remarkable logic, stuck up for herself, even if it was in vain.

Though the time spent on Cape Cod meant we'd be out of school for one week while the rest of the student body had school, we were going to be educated just the same, so I assumed this was why the administration at Perkins had no problem with our outing.

On Sunday afternoon, May 2, 1971, approximately 35 Lower School children, accompanied by their teachers and Mr. Joe, the gym teacher, boarded a bus for the Cape Cod National Seashore in Eastham, Massachusetts. I won't speak for everyone else, but in my opinion, this was the beginning of a week that was unforgettable on many levels. To begin with, boys and girls would be living in the same building, which was yet another upgrade involving the interaction between the sexes outside the classroom. Furthermore, the children would be given additional opportunities to explore the outdoors. Keep in mind that many of us had usable vision, and that's probably why every child who went to Cape Cod was required to bring a flashlight in order to help with his or her exploration.

At 4:00 p.m., we all arrived at our destination. Our living quarters were extremely impressive. We would be spending our week at the Coast Guard station, which had two floors. On the first floor were the girls' bedroom, a sitting room, a kitchen, and a dining room. Upstairs were the boys' bedroom, staff quarters, and bathrooms with showers. Each bedroom had 10 bunk beds. Once all of us became accustomed to our new surroundings and were settled in, we had supper. One of the classes helped prepare the supper, while another class cleaned up after supper.

To pass the time between supper and bedtime, we gathered in the sitting room, where Mr. Joe entertained us. It was then that we realized why Mr. Joe had gone on the trip instead of teaching gym at Perkins that week. He was the entertainment, the social group coordinator, and basically the funny guy on the trip. He talked about a lot of the history surrounding the Cape Cod National Seashore and how it had prospered. Afterward, some of us went outside with our flashlights, trying to make discoveries.

Then it was time for bed. It may have been bedtime, but it wasn't easy to get to sleep. I had 19 roommates, so you can imagine what I had to listen to for an hour or two after the lights went out. Usually, in a crowd of 20 boys, ages 11 through 13, there will be several boys who indulge in extremely graphic conversation. I learned several dirty jokes from these chaps during the Cape Cod trip, which I didn't find too humorous.

On Monday and Tuesday of that week, the weather was cold, cloudy, and damp, which limited us in our activities. We spent most of the time at the house. As usual, one class prepared a meal while another class cleaned up. I remember my friend Alex taking me down to the sand dunes so that I could learn what they were all about. The wind was blowing hard off the ocean that day, helping the dunes grow higher and higher.

While Monday and most of Tuesday were uneventful, things changed in a hurry. There was an incident in the girls' bedroom where one of the bunk beds caved in. Unfortunately, a girl was on the top bunk when it happened, but thankfully, she wasn't injured.

After supper on Tuesday, the children gathered in the sitting room with Mr. Joe for another story. This time, the story had a few twists and turns. As we were sitting in our chairs, Mr. Joe stopped talking. The children began their own conversations while one or two of them approached the sitting room windows. It didn't take long to figure out what was going on. One of the boys, whose name was Buddy, said that an unidentified flying object was in the vicinity of the Cape Cod National Seashore, and though Buddy didn't know why it was there, it was possible that the UFO would invade the area. I didn't take any of what Buddy said seriously. I just sat there and talked.

Soon it became apparent that the conversations about the UFO weren't funny anymore. My classmate Sandra was terrified, and expected the worst. While Sandra was panicking, the story of the UFO became more dramatic, which didn't help matters. After the UFO drama escalated, along with Sandra's fears, Mr. Joe commanded everyone's attention. He wanted to give us an explanation about what was happening. With a voice full of suspense, Mr. Joe told us that the whole story about a UFO was one big, big, big lie, and that we had a few minutes before getting ready for bed. While the children were relieved that the UFO matter was just a hoax, I wonder if Mr. Joe was in on the scheme along with Buddy and his friends. We'll probably never know.

Wednesday was a much nicer day. The sun was out, the wind had died down, and temperatures were much more pleasant than those of the previous two days. There seemed to be more laughter, and spirits were higher. I believe this was the day when we all gathered together for a group picture, which would appear in the Perkins newsletter, *The Lantern*. You can imagine how it must have felt to organize 35 children for one picture. We all gathered near or on the porch stairs of our living quarters. In order for each child to have exposure, the shorter kids had to sit on the bottom stair, while the taller kids either sat or stood behind them.

Wednesday would be the first day that we left the home base to go on a field trip. After we spent the morning entertaining ourselves, we boarded several minivans. Our field trip included a picnic lunch, a tour on a Braille trail, and additional sightseeing. I don't know how we took possession of the minivans, but I assumed the transportation was all prearranged by the planning committee. Finally everyone arrived at the picnic grounds, a few miles from the coastguard station. I don't remember who supplied the food, but I recall how good it was. We all tried to find a comfortable seat to sit on, and soon there was good conversation while we ate our sandwiches, chips, fruit, and whatever else we wanted.

During the picnic, I noticed that one of the girls was acting differently. I had known Lisa very casually for several months, but during this picnic, she decided it was time for me to get to know her much better. She made a point to include herself in my conversations with my friends, something she had never done with me before. She asked me lots of questions, took over the conversation, and became extremely friendly. As if that weren't enough, she decided to pick an acorn off a tree and give it to me as a gift. At that point, I realized what was happening. I was being pursued! I don't know how or why, but at that moment, it didn't matter. I just enjoyed Lisa's attention. After the picnic, we all proceeded to go sightseeing. There I was with the children and staff, proudly hanging onto my acorn, with Lisa still conversing with me.

During this leg of the field trip, my friend Alex accidentally fell in a shallow pond full of mud. The incident was more embarrassing than it was serious. Alex was teased and got mad, but he realized he had a lot of washing up to do when he got back to the coastguard station.

The next place we went was on a Braille trail. The trail was roped off, and at different locations on the rope, there were large signs which described what the landmark at that location was. The words on the signs were in print and Braille and offered an historical synopsis of what we were near. We walked the trail as I listened to instructions from the staff and comments from Lisa.

When the field trip was over, we headed back to the Coast Guard station in the minivans. I rode in a van with Mr. Joe, where he invited all of us to sing goofy songs in order to pass the time while riding back to the Coast Guard station. When we arrived, I proceeded to head for the main door to open it. However, there was no need for me to open the door, because someone was already in the doorway, and I don't think it was a coincidence. I was greeted by Lisa.

Throughout the rest of that day and evening, there was no doubt in my mind that Lisa had taken an interest in me. Was it too good to be true? I don't think we'll ever know, but I found myself bragging to some of the boys about it that night in the bedroom.

The next day, Thursday, I woke up thinking about the events that had taken place the day before with Lisa, and wondered if there would be a repeat performance. Sure enough, Lisa continued to be extremely forward, humorous, and outgoing where I was concerned. She told me her middle name, and then went so far as to give me a nickname. She took my last name, Branco, and elaborated on it. To Lisa, I was now known as "Brontosaurus." At age 13, I was so focused on the fact that a girl had given me a nickname that it didn't matter what Brontosaurus meant: a large, four–footed, herbivorous dinosaur. I'm sure that most people would rather have other pet names than Brontosaurus, but I settled for that name during this rather interesting period on the Cape Cod trip.

On Thursday afternoon, we went on another field trip. Among the places we visited was the city of Provincetown. We walked around the main shopping center and explored other aspects of the city's history. We returned to the Coast Guard station for supper, while I still behaved under Lisa's influence. Like other 13–year–old boys in my day, I was very proud to talk about a girl with my buddies. This was a new experience, and I loved every minute of it.

On Friday, we spent the morning on the Coast Guard station grounds. Then, at 1:00, we boarded the bus back to Perkins, in time for those of us going home for the weekend to meet our transportation.

During the following week, those of us who had gone to Cape Cod settled back into our routine as Perkins students. In my case, I had something else to occupy my mind besides my studies, and that was Lisa. I wondered if her interest in me would go beyond our time on Cape Cod, now that we were back to our old routine. It wasn't long before I found out.

It was a Friday afternoon after lunch, and I proceeded to go to the playground and spend time there before the afternoon school session began. Well, I didn't get very far. I was summoned to the coat locker room where I was given a message. Apparently, Lisa had written me a note, but she knew I couldn't read print. So she had Sandra, my classmate, transcribe it into Braille and deliver it to Potter Cottage. As I read the letter, I was astounded! The letter was full of hatred and name calling. I couldn't figure out why Lisa would write this stuff right after she had chased me all over Cape Cod. Well, there went my dreams of an immediate future with Lisa, because, for whatever reason, she had turned on me.

I can only feel bad for Sandra, writing all these horrible things that Lisa had told her to write. I assumed this because I didn't think Sandra showed hatred the way Lisa did, so I figured Sandra had some compassion. After another note was found on the Potter playground a few days later, one asking me to drop dead and signed by Lisa, I put the whole adventure behind me once and for all.

In the present, I'm in contact with many people with whom I attended Perkins, and at times I talk about the whole Lisa adventure. One guy has a very interesting theory, but of course we'll never know if he's right or wrong. He told me the following: Given the strict rules about boys and girls interacting on campus at the time, Lisa took a huge risk by chasing after me off campus, believing she could get away with it where no one would call her on the carpet. Being that I bragged to many of the kids about Lisa, my friend thinks that word got back to the Glover Cottage staff, and they punished her. If this is true, then I blew it.

Lisa and I are in touch today, but we are just casual acquaintances. I never talk about the incident on Cape Cod, because it doesn't matter anymore. She was 12, and I was 13, and we've done a lot of growing up since. Lisa is a grandmother, and I have a special lady in my life.

Chapter 8

Introduction to the Upper School

When Lower School children reached the end of their sixth–grade year, or when children with special needs were judged to be mature enough, they were transferred to the Upper School. When I realized that I would be heading to Upper School, I had one thought. Most, if not all, of the students would be older than me, at least at first. Many of the friends I had made in Lower School would be left behind, because most weren't in my sixth–grade class. Before I left the sixth grade, I hadn't met very many Upper School students, but occasionally I'd run into one or two if they visited the Lower School or when I used the main gym or swimming pool, which were located in the Upper School. I would also see several older kids during our Boy Scout sessions, or if there was a main event in Dwight Hall for Lower School children to attend, such as a Christmas concert.

I was not afraid of the prospect of going to Upper School. I knew that I would have more freedom there, and that my days of going to bed at 8:30 were over and done with. I had already spent two years on campus, so the prospect of living at school during the week was no longer novel. However, I knew I would be facing several changes in Upper School, and, as it turned out,

I liked most of these changes.

On Monday, September 6, 1971, I was introduced to the Upper School for good. As I describe my new experiences, there is one thing I would like to make note of. My first year in Upper School was also the first year of new leadership at Perkins. The previous director retired, making way for his assistant, Mr. Ben Smith, to take over. I had never met Mr. Smith, and when he became the new director, we all thought that he would pick up right where the previous director had left off, by continuing to enforce the rules on campus that were already in place. As you will read later on in this book, we were all pleasantly surprised by what Mr. Smith did to put an end to the reputation that Perkins previously had, which was that it offered too much of an institutional environment. He was the only visually impaired director that Perkins ever had, and I attended the school throughout his entire administration.

In 1971, Upper School was set up similar to Lower School in one way. That is, the boys were separated from the girls in the cottages, but were allowed to be in every class together, except for gym. The student body consisted of kids from grades seven through their senior year in high school, plus a handful of special needs students who were in the ungraded division. When you entered high school as a Freshman, you were either placed in the college preparatory division, which was also known as the "A" division, or you would be placed in the general course, or "B" division.

The main building of the Upper School was known as the Howe Building, named after a key figure during the founding of Perkins, Samuel Howe. The Howe Building consisted of offices, classrooms, the library, a museum, Dwight Hall, two study halls, the chapel, music practice rooms, the shipping room, the gym, the swimming pool, and industrial arts workshops. The gym area included a wrestling gym, a weight room, a running track, a bowling alley, and another gym for additional recreation and education. The two study halls segregated the sexes. On one side of the building was the boys' study hall, where the boys did their homework at night. The girls had their own study hall on the other side for the same purpose. However, boys and girls were allowed to be in the same study hall during the school day if they had a free period. To put this all in perspective, the theme at Perkins was the same in Upper School as it was in Lower School, and it was left with the previous director's fingerprints all over it, fingerprints that Mr. Smith would soon wipe clean.

On the east and west sides of the Howe Building were two rec rooms. The rec rooms were designed for the students to hang out, have a snack, and socialize. At that time, each rec room was managed by Perkins high school Seniors, under the supervision of a staff member. As you will learn in later chapters, the rec rooms were also the center of a lot of other activity.

There were four boys' cottages located near the east side of the Howe Building: Bridgman, Moulton, Tompkins, and Elliot. Elliot, at the time, was a cottage strictly for deaf–blind boys. On the other side of the Howe Building were six cottages. Brooks, Fisher, May, and Oliver were girls' cottages. Oliver was strictly for the deaf–blind girls. Bennett Cottage was unknown to me at the time, but later it became a cottage of maximum student independence. Keller–Macey Cottage, which later became Keller–Sullivan, grew into a training ground for independent living. I lived in Bridgman my seventh- and eighth–grade years, which were my first two years in Upper School.

After I unpacked that first night, I familiarized myself with Bridgman Cottage. There were a dining room, a sitting room, and a coat room downstairs, and upstairs were bedrooms and a huge bathroom with showers. The sitting room was extremely relaxing. In it were a sofa, a rocker, other chairs, a pool table, a piano, a radio, and a television set. I met many of the other Bridgman boys, who, for the most part, were a lot older than I was. I was also reacquainted with old friends from Lower School, boys that had been in Upper School for a year.

There was one housemother on duty at all times. When the main housemother took time off, her assistant took over. Connected to the cottage was a separate apartment for the housemaster. In my seventh–grade year, the housemaster of Bridgman was an English teacher, Mr. Acres. A few other teachers had their own rooms in Upper School cottages, while the rest of the faculty lived off campus. There was also a cottage captain, usually a responsible student whom the other boys went to for help with internal issues. In all honesty, I never witnessed the cottage captain in action, no matter who he was. Perhaps it's because I never needed his help, or maybe he didn't do his job.

For seventh– and eighth–graders, bedtime in the cottage was at 9:30. Breakfast was served at 7:00 a.m., lunch was at 12:10, and supper was at 6:00 p.m. As was the case in Lower School, the boys in Bridgman were assigned to dish crew on a rotating basis, either after breakfast or after supper.

In seventh grade, my class became more female dominated. Though Sandra stayed back in the sixth grade except for social studies, Jane, Trish, and Liz were promoted with me. Two other girls from Lower School joined my class for the first time, while a newcomer to Perkins, Jennie, became one of the most popular girls on the campus. Not only did she have a terrific personality, but she was creative, funny, and had an intangible presence about her when she entered a room because of her stature. There had never been six girls in my class before, so I felt honored. The two other boys were Juan, a guy who made you laugh because of the way he explained things, and Pedro, a Mexican boy who turned out to be one of my best friends at school. Everett and Albert, who were my classmates in Lower School, stayed behind. As was the case the previous two years, I was in home room for most of my academic subjects in seventh grade. We did have a separate room for social studies, however, but I don't really know why that was. Perhaps the room had maps on the walls, creating a different atmosphere.

I continued with my piano lessons because the principal put piano in my curriculum, along with one period a week of music practice. I remember thinking to myself how flat some of the notes were on a few pianos in these practice rooms, but because of the wonderful piano–tuning department that Perkins had, I knew that these problems would eventually be solved. As you continue to play the piano for a long period of time, you start to hear the flaws in some of the keys, if there are any flaws at all.

Our science class was very traditional, and we participated in a lot of experiments. However, the class took on its own subplot. One day, the science teacher brought two gerbils to class, a male and a female. He put the gerbils in the same cage and asked us to name them. Each one of us chose two names, wrote them down, and put our suggestions in a hat. The winning names were Ozzie and Harriet. Before each science class began, we would check on Ozzie and Harriet to make sure they were well cared for. Everyone fell in love with them, and they became our mascots. One day, it was discovered that Harriet was pregnant, and soon we had a few more mascots.

At Perkins, seventh–graders learned how to use a regular typewriter. However, given the training I had in my New Bedford sight–saving class, I had known how to type since third grade. Just imagine how I felt during my first few weeks in typing class at Perkins, being asked to learn what I'd known for four years. It took everything I had just to hold back in order to play along with the teacher and keep pace with the other students, who were learning how to type for the first time. Months later, when the typing teacher gave us our first speed test, I was clocked at 75 words a minute while the others had just then learned the keyboard. After the others learned, we were all on the same page, no pun intended, and began to do more creative things, like drawing pictures with the typewriter. Using dollar signs, semicolons, periods, colons, and X's, we managed to draw a picture of a Christmas tree and the face of former President John F. Kennedy. We learned how to draw these pictures from a book of instructions.

In Upper School, the gym classes were larger in size. There were approximately 15 boys in my first gym class, and we did everything from performing calisthenics to climbing the Swedish ladder. I was able to handle some of the exercises we were taught, but boy, let me tell you, some of it was extremely difficult and even fearsome. Jumping from a regular bench is one thing, but jumping off a balance beam three feet high and five inches wide is quite another! This requires lots of coordination, confidence, and fearlessness that I did not possess. As we all took turns on the balance beam, several of the boys, along with the teacher, stood on each side, assuring us that we wouldn't fall off.

Sometimes we were afraid of certain things and were able to overcome these fears with a little help and motivation. However, there were times when it appeared as if someone was frightened, but there were other contributing factors which couldn't be avoided. My friend Jack hated the balance beam. Every time he climbed onto it, he was extremely terrified. His fear of the balance beam was well known throughout his class and Bridgman Cottage, so much so that during a Christmas gift exchange, Jack was given a replica of a wooden balance beam, obviously made in wood shop. It had a Braille label on it which said, "Balencia." I'm sure some of the boys thought this was a big joke, but I didn't. One of the main reasons why Jack couldn't handle the balance beam was because of his cerebral palsy.

Many of us at Perkins were part of a pecking order. The wise guys liked to feed off of weaker boys for every reason you can think of. In this case, Jack had a weakness, and one of the tougher boys, who obviously picked Jack's name for the gift exchange, decided to exploit that weakness. As far as I know, Jack did not react to his gag Christmas gift, which was smart, given the pecking order.

In seventh grade, I was introduced to the most boring subject I ever had in my entire school career, ceramics. I'm not criticizing ceramics as a hobby, and I admire what some people do with it. In my case, it didn't take long for me to figure out that I was not one of those people. Every time I attended ceramics class, I always made a pinch pot out of clay. The teacher tried to help, but he and I were never really on the same page. I was not disappointed when ceramics no longer appeared on my class schedule.

I had two other industrial arts courses in seventh grade, wood shop and metal shop. I found metal shop to be slightly more interesting, because the items I made turned out to be quite practical. I remember making a candelabra and a napkin holder for the house, which my mother appreciated. The highlight of my time in wood shop was when I learned how to use the surface planer.

Those of us with coordination problems had additional and more private instruction in a separate class called Corrective Gym, or Motor Training, as it was later called. Among other things, we lifted weights, ran the track, learned how to roller skate at our own pace, and went through obstacle courses.

When I was in the Lower School, I heard about the handbell group, but I never thought I'd ever be a part of it. Sure enough, I was recruited in my seventh-grade year to take part in the handbell ensemble. As people were filing into Dwight Hall to hear the Lower and Upper School choruses perform in the Christmas concerts, the handbell ringers would play several popular Christmas carols. Each member of the group would be given one or two handbells of a different musical note. As we learned the songs, each person was taught when to ring his individual bells in order to make the song work.

In my seventh–grade year, before each school day began, the entire Upper School student body participated in chapel service. At that time, there was still that imaginary line down the middle of the Howe Building, which boys and girls could not cross unless we were in school. The chapel was on that line, so all the girls lined up on the left side of the chapel entrance while all the boys lined up on the right side. During the service, the girls sat together in one section while the boys sat in another. Each morning, we sang a composition which was learned in chorus, along with a hymn directly from the hymn book. Mr. Smith gave a talk, which included notices for the day and week, and then a guest speaker was featured. Normally, chapel service lasted approximately a half hour.

Chapter 9

Mobility Training

Whenever you see a blind person walking through town, he's normally using a cane or a guide dog to help him travel more easily. When I was 13 years old, I had some idea of what guide dogs do, but I had never used a cane. As many of the blind children did, I accepted the fact that we learned how to get around the Perkins campus without a cane or a guide dog, whether we had partial sight or no sight at all.

Prior to my transfer to Upper School, I was introduced to a mobility instructor, who was going to familiarize me with the Howe Building. He gave me a cane for this lesson, but oddly enough, I never needed a cane to travel anywhere on campus throughout all my years at Perkins. It hadn't occurred to me yet just how valuable the cane really is. Today, I don't leave home without it, and looking back, it totally amazes me how children with no sight were able to find their way around the Perkins grounds without the cane. In my case, I depended on my vision to detect landmarks during the day and to locate lights at night.

In Upper School, once I learned my way around most of the campus without a cane, my mobility instructor, Mr. Tyson, taught me simple cane techniques. While walking on paths, you swing the cane in the direction opposite your moving foot. In other words, when you move your left foot forward, you swing the cane to the right, and as you move your right foot forward, the cane swings to your left. This swinging motion creates a protective arc, which includes enough area for you to detect any oncoming obstacles.

As long as I continued with this particular cane technique, I knew when the path turned. Or, if I was following directions, I knew when to make the correct turn onto another path or into a building. Yet, despite all that Mr. Tyson taught me, I put my cane in a coat room at the end of my mobility lesson, where it stayed until my next lesson. This was a habit we all had. Between lessons, we all went about our business, traveling from cottage to school, back to the cottage, and anyplace else on campus without the cane, even in total darkness.

As time passed, I became more confident using a cane on campus, yet I still only used it when I was on a lesson. One day Mr. Tyson decided to put me to the test. He drove me around the school, and at some point, he asked me to get out of the car and find my way back to his office in the Howe Building, given the knowledge I had. This test was known as a campus drop–off. Well, the fact that I had some vision gave me clues. If my lessons were in the morning, and if the sun was in my eyes, I knew I was heading east. If the sun was in my eyes in the afternoon, I was headed west. Most of the time, I was able to find my way back to Mr. Tyson's office, but when I couldn't, he was always following me in his car in case I got into trouble.

The next step in my training was to learn some of the streets around the campus. Crossing the side streets was not a tough task. When I reached the intersection, I lowered my cane in such a way that it was almost lying horizontally against the curb. I listened in both directions for any sound that resembled an oncoming motor vehicle. When it appeared as though no traffic was coming my way, I crossed the side street. When I came to an intersection controlled by traffic lights, the technique was a bit more intense. First of all, it's important to note that the traffic on the street you are crossing is called perpendicular traffic, while the traffic on the street to your side is known as parallel traffic. When I approached the intersection, I lowered my cane in the same position that I described earlier, and was told to wait for the parallel traffic to go. When the parallel traffic was on the move, I was able to cross the intersection, because the perpendicular traffic was faced with a red light and had to stop. At times, I needed to be aware of the possibility that some of the parallel traffic would turn left or right, which means I had to be extremely alert while making my decision to cross the street.

Though these techniques that I learned at school applied no matter where I traveled, the one advantage we had in mobility training was that several of the main intersections near Perkins had audible traffic signals. I guess the town of Watertown installed these audible signals, knowing that a lot of Perkins students would be learning how to cross main streets. These audible signals gave out a ringing or buzzing sound whenever it was time to cross the street. To make sure they worked, I would reach for the traffic light pole and press a button. This would activate the "Walk" and "Don't Walk" feature, and the signal rang when we were allowed to cross. The other option was to stand on the corner and wait. The light would turn red, traffic would stop, and the audible signal was activated.

Several years ago, I led the effort to have audible traffic signals installed at an intersection in New Bedford. In February of 2003, the signals became a reality, though they were financed by private industry instead of by the city itself.

Once I had learned a lot of the geography off campus, Mr. Tyson decided to conduct a more challenging type of campus drop-off. This time, instead of simply driving me around the campus and asking me to find my way back to his office, he drove me off campus, picked a location, and asked me to find my way back. The one thing I should point out here is that the use of my limited vision did play a minor roll in my mobility training, though all my instructors always wanted me to concentrate on my hearing.

The next step in my mobility training was to learn one of the busiest commercial centers in the area, Watertown Square. Without knowing a thing about the Square, one would assume that all it had were simple intersections where a lot of traffic passed through. Well, it wasn't that simple. Much of the square was designed like a rotary, so I had to learn more complex travel methods. The audible signals helped. They were at many of the intersections at the square in order to aid the blind in their travel across some of the busiest intersections in the town.

Many of the Perkins students were cleared by their mobility instructors to go to Watertown Square after hours, but only if the instructors had enough confidence in the particular student's ability to travel to and from the Square without difficulty anytime he wanted. I don't want to mislead you, however. Just because a student was cleared to go to Watertown Square, it didn't mean he went whenever he felt like it. If he wanted to go after supper, he still had to ask permission from his supervising staff member in his cottage. Though most of us who were cleared for Watertown Square had a valid reason for going, some kids, as you will learn later on in this book, got into trouble there. I remember shopping at Bradley's in the Watertown Mall, and at a gift shop to pick out a Mother's Day card.

Once I learned all about Watertown Square, it was time to take the next step toward totally independent travel off campus. At one of the intersections in the Square was a bus stop where we waited for the trackless trolley to arrive. A trackless trolley gets its energy from an electrical wire above it, which means that the route traveled by this particular trolley has to follow the wire. The route that I learned took me directly to Harvard Square in Cambridge, where I got off in the tunnel where the MBTA train tracks for the Red Line were situated. After several trips to and from Harvard Square on the trolley, I learned how to get on the Red Line train. I took the train to Central Square, which was the following stop. Central Square might have been as busy as Watertown Square, but there were no audible traffic signals at the former location. So I had to depend on all the techniques I had learned without expecting a buzzer or a bell to assist me.

Despite all the mobility training I had, I still put my cane away at the end of each lesson and went about my routine without it until the next lesson. It may amaze you to know this; however, most of the students at Perkins felt the same way. I saw a lot of them walk around campus without their canes, and when I had a mobility lesson and picked up my cane in the coat room, there were always a bunch of other canes hanging on hooks near mine. As I said earlier, this was normal. The cane was thought of as a lesson tool, not a tool we used in everyday life. Needless to say, I have a cane now, and I use it every single time I leave the house, no matter what I have to do.

Some of you may be wondering if any of the children at Perkins owned guide dogs. As far as I can remember, I met one high school girl who used a guide dog, and before anyone had a chance to prevent her from using it, they must have realized what the laws were, which allowed this girl to bring the dog everywhere she went.

Chapter 10

Sex, Relationships, and More Changes

I mentioned earlier that Perkins offered a lot of strict rules for children to follow, especially during my first few years there. We quietly complained about some of the rules, because it felt like we were a little too restricted. We knew that it was okay to kiss a girl in public school, and if your parents thought you deserved to stay up past 8:30, you did. There was no strict rule forbidding this behavior at home.

During my first few years at Perkins, when it appeared that the school administrators prevented children from showing certain emotions or having some additional freedom, I felt better when I heard how it was before my time. Sixty years ago, boys and girls were not allowed to be in the same classes together. Girls would help the maid clean the cottage, and all the kids were required to wear something formal to school because of a strict dress code. I later found out while I was in Lower School that the Upper School kids still had to follow the dress code until it was lifted in 1970.

In the Lower School, I didn't learn much about relationships between the opposite sexes, how far these relationships went, and how Perkins controlled what boys and girls did together.

Besides one supper exchange, all I knew in the Lower School was that both sexes were allowed to play together during morning recess, swim in the same pool, and participate in all the classes together except for gym and religion. When the school day was over, a 12–year–old boy did not spend time with a 12–year–old girl until the next day. When I arrived in Upper School, the situation was similar. Boys and girls participated in the same classes except gym, and after school, both genders went their separate ways until the next day, unless they spent time in the rec rooms or joined organizations such as drama club or radio club. During evening study hall time, boys studied with boys, and girls studied with girls, whether they were in their own cottages or the study halls.

In spite of all the restrictions I just described, I found out in Upper School how rules were broken and what form of punishment was handed down. One thing became clear to me and to the administration at Perkins. No matter how hard they tried to put a lid on the students' human emotions or to prevent the students from expressing sexual feelings, these kids found a way around the system. Though campus life was rigid, several girls ended up pregnant and had to leave school. So much for the restriction of sexual availability and ability. I suppose you could say that this was another advantage in learning our way around the campus. Couples found all the hidden locations where supposedly they would never get caught.

Though I didn't take risks in order to express my sexual desires, many students did. In my seventh–grade year, two high school Juniors were caught having sex in the Upper School bowling alley, which was an extension of the gym. The couple was suspended from school. Though the boy never returned, the girl came back a year later. My friend Pedro was dating a girl much older than him, and during his seventh–grade year they fell in love. One day they decided to kiss, and the Dean of Boys found out about it. I don't know if anything was said to the girl, but Pedro was told of the consequences if he kissed her again. As I recall, children who kissed each other at Perkins were suspended from school for a few days.

I never understood the meaning of a school suspension. Was school a privilege that was taken away? I thought school was the main reason we attended Perkins, and the rest of our time took care of itself simply because we had to live there. So taking our education away was punishment? Explain that one to me. I thought punishment meant that you couldn't go to the rec room, couldn't watch television, couldn't go to the Square, or play sports. Whoever heard of skipping school as a form of punishment, when the principal punished kids for skipping school on purpose? It makes no sense.

One change that took place in 1970 was the replacement of religion class with sex education. Because sex education was only offered to the high school students at the time, I missed out in seventh grade. I am only speculating, but I think the addition of a formal sex education course was the solution to a problem recognized by the administration concerning how some of the students spent their free time. I suppose that when a couple was caught having sex, Perkins decided to educate rather than apply a chastity belt. But then again, the school was educating everyone else, because the couple who performed the act were either suspended or expelled. I suppose you could say that I, as a growing teenager, benefited from the sins of Johnny and Suzy.

Though I was only 12 years old when I first heard the boys talk about sex, it wasn't until I was 15 and an eighth-grader that I finally received a formal sex education as part of a class in personal health. At least with a teacher, I learned what I needed to know instead of what the boys wanted me to know, which was how much fun sex is. For two periods a week, the boys had personal health in one room, while the girls took it in another. The two instructors decided in the middle of the school year to teach simultaneous sex education. For three weeks, the boys learned the facts of life in one room, while the girls learned in another. During the fourth lesson, the boys and girls were brought into the same room to discuss what we had all previously learned, and they welcomed questions. I found this to be a very smart move.

It happened to be the only week in the entire school year when both genders took personal health together. Though there may have been a certain degree of embarrassment felt by some of the kids during the joint session of the sex course, we all kept it clean, used words from the dictionary, and came away from class feeling better about ourselves. Though many parents feel that sex education should be taught in the home, some get cold feet and fail to have that elusive talk with their child. With that in mind, I commend Perkins for being proactive in this area: allowing its students to learn all the pros and cons of a sexual relationship, and when the appropriate time for it should be.

Most of the teenage kids that I knew at Perkins had romantic desires, and on numerous occasions, I witnessed episodes of necking and kissing, either in the rec rooms or outside. I wasn't the type to rat anyone out, so I simply turned my back and realized that despite the rules, these teens needed to express their feelings, the same way every other teenager does. Even though the Dean of Boys warned Pedro not to kiss his girlfriend or else he'd be suspended from school, Pedro found opportunities to kiss and neck with her anyway. I would love to talk to a psychologist about what would happen to the average teenager if he or she was held back from expressing their sexual feelings. I'm not necessarily talking about sex, but rather the desire to neck, cuddle, and kiss. In other words, how else would these emotions or desires be channeled if we weren't allowed to express ourselves with the opposite sex on the Perkins School campus?

As for me, I had several crushes on girls in junior high and high school. I tried to impress one girl by telling puns every chance I had, because she used to tell them. I often thought about having relationships, but decided against it for reasons other than what the rules said. My concerns were more geographic. I knew I could get away with kissing a girl on campus, but if a relationship formed, I often thought about what would happen between us after we left Perkins. Many of us lived in different states. What if my girl lived a thousand miles away? Once we finished school, the relationship would be over unless one of us made a very drastic lifestyle change.

During my eighth-grade year, while I had sex education and witnessed all the necking going on around the campus, Mr. Smith instituted a new policy which convinced me that he was well aware of the situation and figured out a way to help us express our romantic feelings. The new policy was known as Cottage Dating. For the first time in the history of Perkins, a boy was allowed to take his girlfriend to his cottage, while a girl could bring her boyfriend to hers. Most of the cottage dating took place in the evening. Being that other people were in the cottages, the dates weren't exactly private. The couples didn't mind. They were just glad to spend time together. This was a new situation, and though they weren't allowed in the bedrooms for obvious reasons, it allowed couples more freedom of expression. Cottage Dating was one of the major moves that Mr. Smith made in order to allow the sexes to relate better to each other. With this new dating policy, there was a clause. When a date was over in the girl's cottage, the boy simply walked back to his cottage. However, when a date in the boy's cottage ended, he had to accompany the girl back to her cottage before doing anything else.

I'm not here to find fault with any of the other Perkins directors, but it was obvious how much Mr. Smith cared about the kids. After all, they are human beings and will act accordingly. Though Pedro's girlfriend was very dominating and controlling, he fell madly in love with her. Deep down, I knew that their relationship wasn't going to last, and it had nothing to do with geography or the rules. Despite how I felt, I also respected the fact that Pedro loved her, no matter how she behaved. Though I more or less knew how he felt, I didn't realize how he really felt until the day she told him she had found another boy.

The conversation, like most others between boys and girls on campus, wasn't private, so other kids, including myself, heard what was said outside one of the rec rooms. While the girl was telling Pedro she was breaking up with him, he began to cry many tears. I eventually took him back to Bridgman Cottage for supper, and noticed that his entire body was trembling. The breakup hit him extremely hard, and it's one of those instances where you can never understand unless you've been through it. You can console and reassure the victim, but it's hard to put yourself in his place. In time, Pedro bounced back, because he had four other girl friends between eighth grade and his high school graduation.

As I mentioned before, Pedro was one of my best friends in the whole school, which meant that I learned how to read him well. He was a smart boy, had a crazy sense of humor, and was extremely sensitive and moody. Being that Pedro was from Mexico, he stayed at Perkins all the time except for extended vacations. I was his roommate three times, so I learned how to size him up. When I came back to Perkins on Sunday afternoons, I often ran into Pedro while I was unpacking my clothes. Quite often, we would discuss our weekends and laugh and joke around.

However, just as often, when I would start a conversation with Pedro, he would give me one-word answers or make a sound like a cow. When I asked him what was wrong, he would either groan or say nothing. It wasn't long before I realized that he had just been in a fight with a girl, and that she had hurt his feelings. I would try to snap him out of it, but he wouldn't cheer up. This drove me nuts. In fact, there were times when he was so upset that his foul mood would last all week, just because a girl had hurt his feelings. Though I know what it's like to be heartbroken, I doubt that I would be a grouch for a whole week. With that said, I wasn't going to be insensitive to Pedro's moods, although they were absolutely intolerable.

With all the dating rules still in place at that time, there were reports that some of the authority figures didn't play along. I heard reports of students having sexual relations with teachers. Am I trying to put Perkins down? No. What I'm trying to say is that stuff happens in a private, institutionalized setting that is common in other settings, and as you will learn later in this book, this was the tip of the iceberg. As Mr. Smith made more changes in Perkins policies, kids were allowed more freedoms. When you are finished reading this book, I would imagine that you would want to compare Perkins before Mr. Smith with Perkins after Mr. Smith, and then you can let me know which environment you would prefer.

Chapter 11

Discipline, Disrespect, and More Changes

During my eight years at Perkins, I tried to be the best student I could possibly be. I spent as much time in the study hall as possible, even when I didn't have to be there. In fact, it got to the point where I was teased for being so studious. Last time I checked, there is nothing wrong with being studious, because you're learning your lessons in order to better yourself. With that said, I was a normal kid, and like any other normal kid, I excelled in many of my subjects while not doing as well in others. I'm proud to admit, however, that the lower grades were not from lack of effort, except in ceramics, which I found extremely boring. I made the honor roll on several occasions, which excused me from mandatory study hall. Though I took advantage of my honor roll privileges on many occasions, I went to the study hall a lot during those times.

I liked and respected most of my teachers, which motivated me even further. If I was late for class, or if I happened to forget or misplace one of my school books, it bothered me a great deal. One day, while I was with Mr. Dees, my guidance counselor, I told him that I had misplaced a book. With all due respect to Mr. Dees because of his credentials, I found him to be a bit cold.

When I told him I had misplaced my book, he accused me of subconsciously wanting it misplaced. But if I was making an effort to be a good student, why would I want to misplace my books, subconsciously or otherwise? Did he think I was a glutton for punishment from my teachers? Did he think I wanted to spend one hour after school in detention? Looking back, I think I should have told Mr. Dees that my subconscious was telling me to miss the next guidance session with him because of his personality. In fact, I only misplaced or lost books three or four times during my school years, but each time was a big deal.

As far as discipline was concerned, teachers had their own rules. While one teacher would send you to detention for being late for class, another would kindly ask you not to be late again. I recall three occasions when I was either late or didn't bring my book, and I got three entirely different teacher reactions.

I'll start out with the most stupid of these reactions. One morning, Juan and I were late for our eighth-grade math class by a few seconds. I can't speak for Juan, but I knew I wanted to be on time, even though Mr. Dees would say I subconsciously wanted to be late. Be that as it may, Juan and I walked into class, and the math teacher, Mrs. La Pointe, decided to make an example of us. She was one of the teachers who lived on the Perkins campus. She lived in Elliot Cottage with her husband, who also taught at Perkins. Being that Juan and I were five seconds late for math that day, Mrs. La Pointe asked us to go to Elliot Cottage at 8:00 that night. She didn't tell us why we had to go there, just that we should go at 8:00.

Juan and I spent the day wondering what Mrs. La Pointe was going to do to us when we arrived at Elliot Cottage. We assured each other that the punishment shouldn't be too serious. After all, we had missed the bell by all of five seconds. At 8:00, I met up with Juan and we casually walked into Elliot Cottage as Mrs. La Pointe had asked us to. When we walked in, there was no one around, so we waited, waited, and waited.

After 10 minutes had gone by, Juan and I left the cottage and thought this was a big joke. The next day, we went to math class as if nothing had happened. We weren't about to ask Mrs. La Pointe why she hadn't been at Elliot Cottage, just in case she had forgotten about it. Apparently she had, because I don't believe that a teacher of her caliber would joke about a punishment.

The second incident also happened in an eighth–grade math class, but with a different teacher, because Mrs. La Pointe had taken maternity leave. The new teacher, Mrs. Stackhouse, was a very refreshing teacher. With all due respect to Mrs. La Pointe, Mrs. Stackhouse appeared to command more respect. She was sharper, more orderly, and at times showed a sense of humor.

One day I was in caning class, where you learned how to cane chairs. I had math class afterwards, and though I usually brought my books to shop in these types of situations, I discovered that I didn't have my math book. After caning class, I ran to the study hall, discovered that my math book wasn't there, and then ran into the principal's secretary's office. When she told me that no one had turned in a lost math book, I ran to Mrs. Stackhouse's class so fast that the gym teachers would have been proud of me. It took five minutes from the time I left caning class, went to study hall, then to the principal's secretary, and then to math. I made it on time, told Mrs. Stackhouse the truth, and didn't get punished.

The amazing part of this story is that I did all of this without bumping into anyone or hitting a wall. I guess when your mind wants your body to do something badly enough, it will do it even though you don't expect it to. I was so driven by my desire to respect Mrs. Stackhouse that all bets were off.

The third incident happened when I was a high school Junior. I was once late for Spanish class because a scheduling quirk bit me in the butt. One year, I started my Friday morning in cooking class, and when it was over, I had to get to Spanish class in five minutes. Well, cooking was in one building while Spanish was in another. Obviously, when you take cooking class, there's the cleanup process.

One day, cleanup took a little longer, so I arrived in Spanish class seconds after the bell rang, meaning I was a bit tardy. When I arrived, the Spanish teacher said, "Buenos días, mangas verdes." While I didn't know what "mangas verdes" meant, I was sure I wasn't in trouble. I asked the teacher to give me the English translation, and she said, "Good morning, green sleeves." I explained why I was late for Spanish that morning, but there was no punishment because my teacher was reasonable about my circumstances.

When it came to discipline, some teachers sent their students to detention after school, which usually took place in the principal's secretary's office. Other teachers gave kids demerits for misbehaving, and when a kid accumulated a certain number of demerits, he or she would either go to detention or perform another service for the teacher. While most disciplinary actions made sense, I questioned others.

One morning, a student was late for chapel line. Being that the boy was late, the teacher in charge asked him to type the entire Bill of Rights. This ridiculous form of punishment must run in families, because it was that same teacher's wife who told Juan and me to go to Elliot Cottage for nothing after we were five seconds late for math class. A Lower School teacher asked his students to remain one minute into their lunch hour each time he caught them practicing a bad habit, such as poking their eyes or rocking back and forth. In case you think this was an acceptable punishment, ask yourself this question. If someone was caught poking her eye 30 times, does she miss lunch altogether? How does it help a student if she misses an entire nutritious meal? Then again, the teacher who kept his students from starting their lunch hour on time was the same teacher who had us make toasted buns without the hot dogs. It makes you wonder if this teacher had a problem with food.

Looking back, I would say that Perkins was like any other school as far as children were concerned, except for the fact that we all had problems with our vision. In my opinion, there were three types of kids: the very nice children, the bullies, and the followers.

Normally, the bullies would get along with each other, but they fed off of other kids' weaknesses. If you reacted to a bully, he would continue to be mean to you. A follower was someone who went with the flow. He hung around with the nicer children when they gave him attention, but when the bullies came around, he'd hang with them, too. I would say that most of the followers had low self–esteem. They wanted attention from everyone, good or bad, rather than picking and choosing a particular group of friends to associate with all the time. Many of the bullies had a short window of opportunity to behave badly. Sooner or later, they would get caught doing something, which usually meant suspension or expulsion from Perkins. The followers were a group that you had mixed feelings about, because if they got into trouble by associating with the bullies, they did one of two things. They either whined about their punishment or they accepted it and changed their attitudes as well as their circle of friends.

I was one of the nicer kids, but at times I tried to befriend followers and bullies because I was also a people person. With that said, I had two character flaws in my teens. I was shy and I felt intimidated. These flaws caused me to be less proactive and less street smart.

One day I decided to go to the study hall, where I knew I would have private time. As I was looking for the study material in my personal cubicle, I found a very obscene letter written in Braille. The contents of this letter were so graphic that I can't repeat them here. After reading the letter, I knew exactly who had written it, based on its tone. Both of these boys were bullies, and one was totally blind while the other had usable sight, so I assumed that the sighted one had dictated the letter to the other for my benefit. Generally speaking, I didn't get along with these two boys at the time, because they knew how I reacted to crap in general, so they continued to irritate me.

While I was reading their grossly obscene letter, I decided to do what was necessary: take it to the Upper School principal. You might say there's nothing wrong with that. Normally, there isn't. However, I chose to confront the boys with the letter first. While I was threatening to take the letter to the principal's office, one of the boys grabbed it and tore it to shreds. I realized then that I should have kept my big mouth shut and simply turned the letter in.

Besides the creation of cottage dating, Mr. Smith made two other major decisions in my eighth–grade year. As you know, we used to start every school day in chapel. Mr. Smith cut chapel from five to three days a week, while we reported to study hall on the other two days for roll call. The number of school periods per day increased from eight to nine. With this new arrangement, there was a period on Friday where most of the Upper School kids ended up in study hall. During this period, a majority of the faculty had meetings.

While this appears on the surface to be normal, it ended up being the perfect storm for trouble. If most of the teachers were in meetings, and if the only students who didn't have a study hall period were on the honor roll or had glee club or piano practice, then the result was an overcrowded study hall with no supervisor. You may feel that this was okay. After all, we were teenagers, and as long as we had homework to do, why should we care if there was a supervisor or not? But think again. A lot of students did not spend time in the study hall to do homework, and if there wasn't a supervisor on duty to control the rowdy bunch, then this bunch took control. They talked with one another while the studious ones tried to do their homework.

When several of the serious students got mad at the talkers, one thing led to another until fights broke out.

My friend Albert, who had a bad temper when teased, was trying to study. The bullies who were having conversations knew this, so they began to tease him. At one point, Albert picked up a Braille machine and threw it at the head of one of the bullies, missing by mere inches. While this was going on, several other students were wrestling and pushing one another against the wall. Still other groups of kids exchanged vulgar language. This type of behavior didn't happen just once, but many Fridays during this period. I found it impossible to do my homework.

As I observed this behavior in the study hall, I asked myself what possessed these kids to act that way. I suppose I could blame the administration for not anticipating this, but then again, if I had been part of that administration, I would have assumed that teenaged boys would show more respect, even though the study hall was unsupervised. Let's face it. It was no longer a study hall. It was a zoo.

Eventually, I was assigned to piano practice during that period, so I escaped from the zoo in order to concentrate on Mozart. I hardly ever went back to study hall during this period, so I don't recall how this nonsense got resolved. I would hope that someone was allowed to leave the staff meeting in order to supervise, because I do know that the principal eventually learned about the study hall free–for–alls.

Chapter 12

Sports, Socials, and Recreation

In Upper School, our day in class was as long as in Lower School, but instead of having free time for an hour between the end of school and suppertime, many of us were required to take part in after-school sports. These sporting events were usually held two days a week for about half the school year. The kind of sports we participated in depended on the season. In the fall, we were involved in cottage baseball, bowling, or track and field activities. In the winter, our options were swimming, apparatus, wrestling, or weight lifting. In March, there was more bowling and several other activities, but as the spring approached, the after-school sports were not a priority as they were earlier in the school year. It's true that some of the kids signed up for track and field in order to participate in scheduled track meets, so they worked very, very hard all year round, either after school or during gym classes.

Cottage baseball was extremely competitive. It was not as accessible to the blind as modern-day Beep Ball is, except for two things. In a Perkins baseball game, the pitcher was encouraged to throw to the hitter on a bounce, so that the hitter knew when it was time to swing the bat. You would be surprised at how far some of the totally blind players hit the ball. The second thing that helped a blind person play baseball was when the opposing infielders would call the base runners to a particular base. I remember one time when that didn't happen to me. I hit a ball, ran to first base, and collided with a big boy on the opposing team.

At first, cottage baseball consisted of the boys' cottages in one league and the girls' cottages in another. As the years went by, the sport became coed, meaning that boys and girls played together. On numerous occasions, the baseball games had a public address announcer, usually the Upper School principal.

The baseball games were normally played on a baseball diamond in the Perkins athletic field. The athletic field was cleverly constructed. Around the baseball diamond, the basketball court, and the swings was a running track, where kids would run, walk, or jog, either at their convenience or during lengthy sprints at track meets. There was also a smaller running area for 50–yard dashes, which included a guard rail for blind kids to follow with their hands. When we participated in track and field, some of the exercises we did included the 40– and 50–yard dashes, the football throw, the football kick, the broad jump, and the shot put. Those of us who weren't very athletic simply benefited from these activities, while the more athletic boys and girls participated in track meets with other schools in the area.

At times, we ran the indoor track, and we looked forward to breaking our own personal running record. While it normally took me one minute and 15 seconds to run four laps around the indoor track, which was a little more than a sixth of a mile, other kids would do it in less than a minute. There were embankments on each of the turns, so that we could build momentum as we ran. Sometimes we were asked to do more extensive running, such as the half mile, which took approximately 11 laps. In order not to get too tired, I used to jog the first eight laps, and then pick up speed during the last three.

Another very important track and field event which many kids prepared for was the high jump. Admittedly, I was not very good at it, but I watched in amazement as other kids cleared the bar at five and six feet. Jennie, whom I referred to earlier as the most popular girl at Perkins, was a pure athlete. She finished first in many track and field events for the girls, and later on, after she graduated from Perkins, I learned that she joined Special Olympics. One night, she appeared on a Boston newscast as well as in a local newspaper because of her outstanding abilities as an athlete. Many kids participated in track and field events, track meets, after–school sports, or regular gym class, but out of all those kids, Jennie was the most enjoyable to watch as she did the high jump. If I'm not mistaken, she once cleared the bar at six and a half feet.

Though I always followed the four professional sports of baseball, basketball, football, and hockey, the sport I excelled at the most was bowling. In the Upper School, the boys and girls had separate bowling tournaments, which were organized by the gym teachers. These were double–elimination tournaments, where the top three bowlers received gold, silver, and bronze medals respectively. A double–elimination tournament is one where you have to lose two bowling matches before you are eliminated from further competition. It was candlepin bowling, which is unique to New England and the Canadian maritime provinces. We used a small ball to try to knock all 10 pins down in three tries.

The gym teachers had another important task on their hands. Since some bowlers had more sight than others, the teachers had to figure out a way to run the tournaments as fairly as possible. Their method proved to be a bit controversial in my eyes. Because some of us had more vision than others, we were placed in two divisions, the blind and the sighted. I was placed in the blind division, though I was able to see the bowling pins and the ball as it was rolling down the lane. I don't feel that the physical education department clearly understood how complicated it was to put us in just two divisions, because every individual student had his or her own degree of visual limitation. For example, many kids had a lot more sight than I had, while others had no sight at all. If I had been put in the sighted division, I would probably have been overmatched, but on the other hand, as someone who could see the pins, I had an advantage over most of the bowlers in my division.

However, there was nothing I could say to help make the bowling tournaments be run any more fairly than they were, because there really wasn't any solution to recommend. So there I was, with my limited sight, bowling in the blind division, while the sighted kids bowled in theirs. I'm sure I wasn't the only bowler with this predicament, as other kids had vision similar to mine. In one bowling tournament, I received the bronze medal, while in another, I got the silver. I was very honored to receive these awards, which I won under a system which seemed acceptable to both the faculty and the bowlers. For this reason, I didn't feel guilty at all.

Most of us who went swimming after school probably found it a bit boring, except those who loved to show off their diving skills. There was a strange, unwritten rule in the sports program about how to leave the swimming program to join another winter sport. Unless you proved to the instructor that you could do one lap around the pool without stopping, you supposedly could not join weight lifting or apparatus. I think the wrestlers were the exception, because the recruitment process was different for them. Since I wasn't a wrestler and was not very good with the apparatus, I either swam or lifted weights.

It wasn't until high school that the trampoline became a part of my life in after-school sports. This was something I could handle and had fun with. Moving on a trampoline makes you feel lighter than you actually are, because of how it's constructed with the springs underneath. For safety reasons, there were always spotters on each side of the trampoline in case something serious happened. Though I was careful on the trampoline, there were a few kids who wanted to prove just how macho they were when performing a physical activity. One day in gym class, while we were spending time with the trampoline, something very rare but exciting happened. Everyone took their turn, until a big guy who was also a member of the wrestling team decided to make the most of his huge ego. He moved around on the trampoline with tremendous aggressiveness. Suddenly, as he was showing off his macho character, we heard a loud *snap!* One of the springs on the bottom had let go, meaning that our trampoline practice was cut short rather abruptly. The guy jumped off, a bit embarrassed by the situation.

Though I wasn't a member of the Perkins wrestling team, I attended many of the matches that it had with other schools, as long as the matches were at Perkins. While our wrestlers faced off against rival schools, our cheerleaders performed their routines to motivate our team.

Another part of the Perkins curriculum which gave us an opportunity to socialize was the integration with students from other schools. Perkins had a social activities coordinator, who organized social mixers so that the blind and sighted could interact. We would spend time with kids from either secondary school or college. While I didn't attend many of the social mixers, I will talk about a few noteworthy events which I did attend.

The first was a bowling event. I recall some of the Upper School boys spending a Thursday evening with sighted girls from a local junior high school. The event was informal, but that didn't matter. The purpose was not to find out who bowled better. It was all about integration with the outside world. As we all began to bowl, I realized how important this type of event was to us, because it expanded our horizons. Though we all lived together as a blind community, we knew that life wasn't going to be this way once we were out of school.

When we all realized that our bowling mixer wasn't formal, a few of the sighted girls took full advantage of the situation. It was my turn to bowl, so I threw the ball down the alley and probably knocked half the pins down. Suddenly, while my ball was headed for the pins, another ball followed it. I was an old school chap, so, despite the fact that this was an informal event, I didn't take too kindly to having my bowling score tainted. After this happened the first time, I asked why, but didn't get an answer. My turn came again, so I threw the ball down the lane, only to see a second ball follow! This time, I realized that the second ball had come from behind me and had rolled between my legs. When I bowl, I use an open stance, which helps me with my balance and direction. When I asked where the second ball had come from, I was told that one of the sighted girls was enforcing my score. At first I thought how unfair it was, but then I let it slide, given the nature of this mixer. We were supposed to have a good time with girls from other schools, not compete for awards.

In my Sophomore year of high school, the social coordinator, in collaboration with the physical education department, organized a month–long activity in which Perkins and college students partnered up in order to explore our personal environment in the form of exercise and the knowledge of the human body. Before your mind wanders toward the gutter, allow me to explain that this was a weekly event, combining social interaction, sports, and gym. It was called Creative Movement. I wasn't sure if the Perkins girls participated in Creative Movement, but I remember boys partnering up with college girls.

Creative Movement did not take place in the gym, but rather in the North Building. This activity wasn't tiresome, and it gave us an opportunity to get to know our bodies while using our minds. Though Creative Movement was an extracurricular activity during the period when many of the rigid campus rules were changing, I'm willing to bet that this event would never have taken place before Mr. Smith became the director of Perkins. Do you honestly believe that any previous director who didn't want his own boys and girls to hold hands would want teenaged boys and college girls to interact on a gym mat, even if the activity appeared to be clean and aboveboard? I sincerely doubt it!

If we needed extra reading done, especially of library books obtained off-campus as part of research projects, the Perkins social program offered volunteers from colleges to read to us. Quite often, we couldn't find research material on campus, so we had to apply for a card for the Watertown library in order to get our work done. Unlike the books at the Perkins library, those in the Watertown library were not in Braille.

Chapter 13

Clubs and Organizations

As I hinted earlier, Perkins kept us very busy, even if we weren't in school or doing homework. There was always something for us to do. Some of the extracurricular activities were required by the school, while others were optional. The required activities usually included the sports, chorus rehearsals, and handbell rehearsals. Why do I call them required, you ask? Well, if our teachers asked us to get together after school, we had to. If we were in the chorus, then evening rehearsals were part of it. Don't get me wrong. We didn't spend the entire year rehearsing at night. There were two periods in the school year when the chorus sang in concerts, December and May. In December, we sang in three Christmas concerts, and in May, the concert normally consisted of a famous Broadway musical, requiring extensive planning and rehearsal.

As I became more involved with required nighttime activities outside of our normal study routine, it became quite obvious that each teacher had his or her own agenda, and it appeared as though there was no consideration for what any of our other teachers wanted us to do. When our chorus teacher scheduled evening concert rehearsals, I'm sure he didn't consider the fact that most of us had homework to do in English, math, or any other academic subject. It would be our job to figure out an alternative time to study so we could work around the chorus rehearsals.

There was also no regard for our bedtime, a bedtime required by the cottage staff. If a chorus rehearsal ran until 11:00 p.m., an hour past our high school bedtime, then so be it. It would have been interesting, however, to find out who won the power struggle between the chorus teacher and any other authority figure who handed down rules which conflicted with rehearsal time.

On one occasion in my Junior year of high school, at a point in the year where I found myself a bit overwhelmed, I actually asked my mother to write a letter to Mr. Smith, insisting that I be excused from chorus. He ignored the request, so I simply accepted the decision and lived with it. It wasn't as if chorus rehearsal or any other activities were difficult. They were just time–consuming. With that said, and given the fact that there were only 24 hours in a day, I had deep admiration for any student who filled his or her day with multiple activities. Jennie, the most popular girl at Perkins at the time, juggled a list of activities so impressive that it nearly gives me the chills to think about how busy she was, given our restrictions. During a typical high school year, Jennie had the following activities outside of class: class president, glee club member, drama club member, chorus member, participant in the Perkins Athletic Association, babysitter for staff members' children, participant and volunteer helper during after–school sports, and possibly a member of the Perkins student council. I wonder if I missed anything.

Though we had a lot of fun in handbells, we were required to have separate rehearsals for those in the same manner as for chorus, because most of the concerts we participated in had a handbell segment. As with chorus, the handbell rehearsals took up time that we normally would have spent doing our homework.

Several students had a passion for amateur radio. For this reason, a radio club was formed, where students would meet once a week to learn Morse code and to check out two–way radios, which were common at the time. For several weeks in my eighth–grade year, I decided to go to radio club meetings. It was a great experience, though I wasn't passionate enough to pursue an amateur radio license yet. During the 1970s, you were required to learn Morse code in order to receive your first license. Ironically, it wasn't until 2003 that I became a licensed amateur radio operator, and by that time, the Morse code requirement had been lifted. Not only did Perkins produce blind amateur radio operators, but there are many licensed blind people in today's society who enjoy the hobby.

One organization that I regretted not joining was the Perkins student council. Though I wasn't part of it, I want to mention it because of its worth to the school. A group of several students, most of whom were representing their cottages, met once a month to propose and discuss student policies to be approved by the faculty and administration. The members of the student council were elected by their peers.

I suppose that if you wanted to consider the cottages club houses, their residents could have been considered organizations, because at times they would have their own meetings with the cottage captain. There were times, though very infrequent, when the cottage residents and staff felt that a meeting was necessary to iron out differences or simply to remind us of our responsibilities in the cottage. Every boy in my cottage had at least one responsibility, starting in the bedrooms. Each boy would take turns with his roommates mopping the bedroom floor for a week at a time. Each boy in his bedroom would take turns emptying the trash from the bedroom to the main trash bin downstairs. Each boy in the cottage would take turns cleaning up after a meal, either by sorting silverware or washing dishes and silverware in the automatic dishwasher. Also, one of the boys in the cottage would collect sheets and pillowcases from each bedroom once a week and put them all into a big laundry bag for the cottage staff to wash.

When we became high school Freshmen, our class, like other high school classes, raised its own funds for future activities, such as a fair or a Senior trip. Thursday afternoons were when clubs and organizations met after school. Usually there were four organizations that took turns meeting: the Perkins Athletic Association, the student council, the drama club, and our class meetings. That way, if you wanted to be really busy, like Jennie, you'd be out every Thursday after school, devoting your time to four organizations in a coordinated schedule.

Our classes met once a month. We elected a president, vice-president, secretary, and treasurer, while being advised by two members of the faculty who normally attended the meetings. Jennie was elected president for four years, which shouldn't have surprised anybody who cared. Based on tradition, the Freshmen would usually hold a car wash while the Sophomores sold Christmas cards, the Juniors ran their own fair on the Perkins campus before summer vacation, and the Seniors had their prom and took a trip to Washington.

My class honored most of that tradition, but we also had to do things a little differently because of unforeseen circumstances. We held our Freshman car wash in our Junior year, and I didn't go to Washington as a Senior.

I don't remember much about the car wash, probably because I wasn't there. I heard that it rained a little that day, but no one ever talked about it much in class. Though I didn't participate in the car wash, I was very much involved in the card sale, and we did raise a little more money for our treasury.

Since my seventh–grade year, I had been to several Junior

fairs, and I enjoyed myself to the fullest. Each year, the Juniors ran the fair two days before the end of school, and it was always held on the campus. The students would set up vending stands, a hay ride, and other fun activities. Some fairs were better than others, but no matter what, I always knew that students put their heart and soul into the fair every year. During my first experience at a Junior fair, I had a buffalo burger for the first time in my life. To this day, I don't know why they called it a buffalo burger, because it tasted like a regular hamburger as far as I was concerned.

The one thing that I will always remember most about my first Junior fair was the girl at the vending stand. For the balance of the afternoon, she kept shouting out the same list of foods over and over: "Hot dogs! Hamburgers! Cheeseburgers! Pepperburgers! Subs!" It's a wonder that I didn't pig out after hearing the names of these delicious foods repeated again and again.

When I became a Junior, it was time for me to help run the fair rather than simply going to it and having fun. I remember spending most of that morning carrying items to the fairgrounds. During the fair itself, I was the ticket guy who sat by the gate with a cash box and tickets on a small table. Though most people who attended the fair were from Perkins, outsiders were allowed admittance as well, or so I thought.

While I was selling tickets, two young boys, ages nine and 10, saw what I was doing and approached me. The boys were totally sighted and lived off campus, but they seemed interested in going to the Junior fair. I told them that they needed to give me their money before I could give out the tickets, but they wanted me to give them the tickets first, with the condition that they would go home and get the money. In a stern voice, I insisted that I would not allow them in the fair without their money, and as soon as they brought it back from home, I'd give them the tickets. The boys left, never to be seen again.

After a while, Jennie, the class president, came along, took the cash box, and relieved me of my fair duties, because I was working very hard. That evening, we ran an outdoor block dance, but I was told just to relax and have a good time there.

I had some of my most exciting times at Perkins while in drama club. Mr. Acres, the English teacher I referred to earlier, ran the club, and each year he put on two performances, a Christmas skit in December and a major play in the spring. The Christmas skit was always taken from an actual play or movie, only Mr. Acres changed it in order to add more humor. During my four years in drama club, I remember being in three Christmas skits, while in my Senior year, I had the honor of reading the Santa letter to the audience. The letter asked Santa to give gifts to students and staff that a particular committee felt were appropriate, based on their personalities, habits, and tastes. For example, we had a friend who loved milk, so the letter asked Santa to give the boy his own personal cow.

The four major spring performances that I participated in were as follows: *My Favorite Haunts*, *In Case of Murder*, a major Bicentennial celebration combined with the chorus, and *Night of January Sixteenth*. I had only a small part in *My Favorite Haunts*, but I found the play rather eventful in spite of my lack of involvement. However, I had a more major role in the play *In Case of Murder*. I played the part of a rich psychotic. I not only had to memorize more lines than ever before, but I also learned how to put all my trust in my fellow actors and actresses.

During one scene, it had to appear as though I was knocked unconscious with a paperweight. When I was found, three girls and a guy had to carry me into a closet: one person at my feet, one at my left hand, one at my right hand, and one at my head and shoulders. They put me in the closet, stood me against the door, and closed it. That wasn't the best part. Moments later, a girl who played the part of a male police officer had to open the closet door. Being that I was still supposed to be unconscious while leaning against the inside of the door, I had to fall forward when she opened it, hoping she'd prevent me from falling all the way onto the floor. Thank God she had a lot of vision! Though I was nervous about that scene, it received a ton of laughs, so I felt better about doing it.

Though this scene could have been very embarrassing had it not worked out, it would not have been nearly as embarrassing as what happened prior to the dress rehearsal before we left the makeup room. I'm sure you've all heard the expression "Break a leg," which means "Good luck." Before we all went backstage for the dress rehearsal, Mr. Acres told us to break a leg. It just so happened that while one of the actresses was walking down the stairs from the makeup room to the backstage area in Dwight Hall, she fell and nearly did break her leg. She was on and off crutches for the next week or so, including times during the play.

The Bicentennial musical, which the drama club and chorus collaborated on, included music and scenes from our country's first 200 years like you've never seen before. There were scenes from the Revolutionary War, comments from the old railroad days, camping songs, highlights from the industrial revolution, and a trip through the first 70 years of the 20th century. The musical was two and a half hours in length, with lots of rehearsal time. Remember that we still had to do our homework no matter what.

The play *Night of January Sixteenth* had two different endings, because the play centered around a murder trial and an actual jury's decision. Jurors were picked from the student body and the faculty to sit in a makeshift jury box during the play. Their job was to hear the evidence and decide whether the defendant was guilty or not guilty. Being that we didn't know how the jury was going to vote during the actual play, we had to learn both endings. On the first night of the performance, the jury voted one way, and on the second night, a different jury voted the other way.

Chapter 14

A Closer Look at Mr. Smith

As you've probably gathered by now from the material you've read so far in this book, Perkins, prior to Mr. Smith's administration, was thought of as an institution where students had to abide by strict traditions, such as early bedtimes, no kissing, proper dress codes, study hall every night, the boys and girls living in separate cottages, five days of morning chapel service before school, and one hour of religion every week. I've already mentioned two notable changes in the policies at Perkins before Mr. Smith took over as director in 1971, which were the termination of the dress code and religion being replaced by sex education for the high school kids. Though I had mixed feelings about the termination of the dress code, I was completely in favor of sex education, but I don't think it should have replaced religion.

Regarding the influence that Mr. Smith had on Perkins, I saw it all, because I was at Perkins during his entire administration. He took over as director in 1971 and left when I graduated in 1977. I also implied that Mr. Smith was a reactionary director, observing things on the inside while dealing with legislative changes on the outside. From the inside,

I will assume that the student council played a very small role in what Mr. Smith did, if he believed that the requests from the council were reasonable.

Looking back, I place all of Mr. Smith's executive decisions into three categories. There were the decisions he had to make based on legislation, decisions that he made because of changes in society, and things which I have yet to figure out.

I'll start with his decisions that I haven't figured out.

During his second year as director, Mr. Smith cut morning chapel service from five days a week to three days a week, and then to two days a week the following year.

As class sizes were getting smaller through the mid 1970s, there was a concern about the size of the chorus. Chorus was usually held in the chapel, and it became apparent that there was a lot of extra room on the benches. In my opinion, Mr. Smith, with help from the chorus director and the upper school Principal, solved that problem by being *too* proactive. Kids were asked to join the chorus without taking voice lessons. I know this for a fact because I was placed in the chorus in my Freshman year without having taken a voice lesson.

Though I am no Frank Sinatra myself, I knew my friends well enough to have knowledge of their singing abilities. Those who couldn't sing not only knew they couldn't, but they grew very bored with chorus and made fun of it. To me, a good chorus is better off with quality, not quantity. I don't know what possessed the Perkins administration to dump kids who had no singing voice into the chorus, but it happened. One kid thought he knew exactly how to get out of chorus without going through a lot of red tape. He simply broke the chapel bench.

A third change that Mr. Smith instituted that I can't figure out was the lifting of evening study hall requirements for students who were not on the honor roll, except for those students who had a C or lower in one or more of their major academic subjects. With the type of schedule we had in Upper

School, the evening study hall period was an ideal time for most of us to do our homework. Though I liked having the option of not going to evening study hall as long as I didn't get a C, I went there a lot, because that was the best time for me not only to do my homework, but to discuss it with any other classmates who happened to be in the study hall with me. There was a little free time during our school schedule for us to go to study hall, but with the number of academic subjects most of us had, you really couldn't do all the homework during the day, and I wasn't one to bring homework to the cottage or home on the weekend. Don't get me wrong. I understood why kids who made the honor roll didn't have to go to study hall every night, because that was an earned privilege. I also understood why those of us who received C grades had to be there. It's that middle ground that made no sense, given our lives at Perkins.

I'm now going to talk about several of Mr. Smith's administrative policy changes that I believe were made because of society or because I felt they made a lot of sense. I'll stick to the concept of study hall for the moment. While he lifted the requirements for students to attend evening study hall every night unless they had a C or lower in one or more of their academic subjects, girls were now able to attend evening study hall with boys. Both sexes met in the boys' study hall, and I don't remember what purpose the girls' study hall served as of this change.

In my second year in Upper School, the number of class periods per day increased from eight to nine, with five minutes cut from each period to make room for the additional period at the end of the day without affecting the time we got out of school. There were new classes added to the curriculum at the time, which justified the increase in the number of school periods. These new classes included home and personal management, salesmanship, and Optacon.

Home and personal management focused on cooking,

although other aspects of independent living were included in the course. Salesmanship spoke for itself. Most of the high school students in the B division took it as a career opportunity, along with business math, office practice, and transcription.

The Optacon, which was introduced in 1972, was one of the first scanners of print material. A small camera was attached to a box. On the front part of the box was a small rectangular space for your index finger. Inside this space were a number of pins which vibrated when the camera saw something to read. With the opposite hand, you would manually move the camera across the print page while combinations of pins would form the vibrating letters under your index finger, the letters that the camera saw. To help the instructor determine how you were performing, the Optacon had a small television box which viewed the letters you were scanning with the camera. Keep in mind that in 1972, this device fascinated us, because there weren't any talking scanners yet. We were just so amazed to read the phone book, newspaper articles, and other print documents with the Optacon. I took the course for several weeks, and managed to read at a speed of 10 to 15 words a minute. In comparison, the best Optacon students read at a rate of 35 words per minute.

I previously mentioned how the boys and girls took gym classes separately. During Mr. Smith's administration, coed gym was introduced, though the boys and girls continued to go to their separate locker rooms to change and take their showers. Though I had no problem taking gym with girls, the first two or three times were challenging. The male and female gym instructors worked together, along with one or two trainees, and we managed to do the same things that we normally did in the past. However, as our first year of coed gym went by, we played a sport that males and females play together on a regular basis, volleyball.

As I stated earlier, Keller–Sullivan Cottage became the

training headquarters for independent living. As some of the students became more self-sufficient, they spent several weeks in that cottage, making their own meals, doing other chores, and having additional freedom. It was usually a five-week learning experience before they headed back to their original cottages, but if a student progressed further, he or she actually spent more time in Keller-Sullivan, even as long as an entire semester. I lived in Keller-Sullivan for five weeks prior to graduation, which I will discuss in detail later.

In a previous chapter, I mentioned the two rec rooms that adjoined the Howe Building, one on the east (boys') side, and one on the west (girls') side. Each rec room was long and narrow, with a sofa, vending machine, radio, and other minor essentials which helped students in a social setting. In 1973, a larger rec room was built on the east side of the Howe Building. This brand-new facility had several tables and chairs, vending and soda machines, a radio, and a larger store, where other foods were sold. This rec room became the center of social activity when the students were free, and many more students congregated in the new rec room than they had in both of the older and smaller facilities.

While it was common sense that this larger rec room was the place to go for food, drink, and conversation, there were occasional moments when sex might have been thought of. I remember walking into the rec room once, and there, on the floor, were a high school boy and a deaf-blind girl in the middle of foreplay. When they became aware of me, they stopped.

On one occasion, the rec room was used for a major school activity. I don't recall if the activity was organized by one of the high school classes or the social coordinator, but a record hop took place one evening with Top 40 music and snacks. Everyone was invited.

I would now like to talk about the policy changes that Mr. Smith introduced to Perkins based on legislation and other outside influences, as opposed to changes he made from within and with assistance from the student council. In the mid–1970s, legislation was passed in Massachusetts which allowed blind students more of an opportunity to be mainstreamed in public school. The legislation, known as Chapter 766, created a huge domino effect at Perkins, resulting in a total makeover of the school, making way for what Perkins is today. A number of students who had been at Perkins, either for a little while or since kindergarten, left to go to public school. As a result, class sizes grew smaller and smaller.

Prior to 1975, the average size of a graduating class at Perkins was approximately 25 students. As a result of Chapter 766 and students leaving to go to public school in their home states other than Massachusetts, class sizes dwindled to 15 in 1975 and 1976, and to 10 in 1977, which was my graduating class. Mr. Smith needed to do something about this trend very quickly if Perkins was to continue operating on some level.

Before I mention the new direction that Perkins had to go in, I will explain what Mr. Smith did as a result of Chapter 766, though some of what he did wasn't totally necessary. When I first came to Upper School in 1971, students had the option of taking one of three foreign languages: Spanish, French, or Latin. By the time I entered my Freshman year in 1973, which was about the same time Chapter 766 came into being, Latin had been dropped from the curriculum, and then eventually French followed.

As more students were leaving Perkins before graduation, Mr. Smith was faced with another dilemma. How was he going to fill the spaces in all the Upper School cottages? Prior to the fall of 1973, there were three cottages for the boys: Moulton, Bridgman, and Tompkins, and three cottages for the girls: Brooks, Fisher, and May. There were other cottages for the deaf and for independent living, but we'll leave them out of this discussion for the moment.

In September of 1973, the girls in Fisher Cottage were moved to Brooks and May, while the boys from Bridgman Cottage moved to Tompkins and Moulton. The move to the other cottages helped to fill some of the spaces created by the exodus of students, while Fisher and Bridgman became the focal points for two new programs introduced by Mr. Smith. The new programs served as a turning point for the school on three levels. First, more blind students with other special needs were allowed to come to Perkins. They lived in Fisher, along with several junior high and ungraded kids. Second, many older blind students, and those who had previously graduated from Perkins or other schools, were allowed to participate in an adult rehab program in Bridgman. Third, both Fisher and Bridgman became the first two cottages in Upper School with boys and girls living together.

As you think about this, just remember the strict rules which kept boys and girls from expressing their feelings for one another. Don't let anyone kid you about these new coed situations. Do you honestly think that boys and girls did not visit each other's bedrooms? Trust me, I heard detailed accounts of things that happened in those bedrooms. One night, a boy had to hide his girlfriend in the closet while someone stopped by his room in order to check up on him. I wonder if these types of occurrences ever crossed Mr. Smith's mind, or did he actually have faith in these boys and girls that they would abide by the previous rules? This is a subject for much debate. If boys were allowed to visit other boys' bedrooms in order to hang out with their friends, then why couldn't boys visit girls' bedrooms in the newly formed cottages that the director of Perkins had created?

While grade school students continued to leave Perkins, a new bunch of students arrived, most of whom were from New Jersey. While I didn't know at the time why New Jersey was sending Perkins a lot more students, I later found out that the New Jersey Commission for the Blind had launched a special campaign to refer students to Perkins. The details of this campaign were mentioned to me, but I don't quite remember specifics.

Most of the new crop of students were not college bound, and some were best suited for rehab and/or independent living programs. In 1975, two years after he put boys and girls together in Fisher and Bridgman Cottages, Mr. Smith had another decision to make based on the new influx of students. As Perkins became less of an academic school, more and more cottages had boys and girls living together. I never understood the connection between the trend toward fewer academic subjects and more coed cottages, but Mr. Smith must have felt he had a reason for doing what he did.

When Bridgman and Fisher became coed in 1973, I was transferred to Tompkins. In 1974 and 1975 respectively, Brooks and Tompkins became coed as well, meaning that all the Tompkins boys and Brooks girls had to move in order to make room for the additions to the new programs that had been put in place earlier. In fact, Tompkins prepared many young blind adults for community residence. Grade–school boys had only two choices at this point. Either they went to Moulton, or they went to yet another brand–new independent living facility on campus called the Northeast Building. Even the Northeast Building, after several years of having just boys in it, added girls in 1976, which meant that a total of four regular Upper School cottages and three independent living cottages were coed by the time Mr. Smith retired in 1977, the year I graduated.

The point to this discussion is that society played a major role in dictating how Perkins needed to prepare for the future. It was changing its identity. What was once a completely academic school for the blind with strict rules was slowly but surely becoming a training ground for independent living and additional career opportunities. By 1975, there were approximately 20 boys and 20 girls in the entire Upper School who had plans for college, while everyone else concentrated on a career, such as salesmanship, switchboard work, office practice, piano tuning, home economics, transcription, and receptionist work. The girls took sewing, housekeeping, and knitting.

Work experience was also introduced into the school curriculum. In my Sophomore year, I worked two periods a week in the research library and got credit for it. I answered the phones, copied documents, and did some other odds and ends for the research librarian. In my Senior year, my transcription class had a contract with WGBH Television. WGBH would send the transcription teacher copies of their interview programs, and we were paid to transcribe the programs into hard copy, in case a viewer requested a transcript of a particular show.

Like any other school director, Mr. Smith had his supporters and his opponents. Looking back, I believe he had many more supporters than opponents, just because he allowed the student body more options and more flexibility than it had ever had before. His support also extended beyond Perkins, to the point where he received financial support that he had never expected.

In the 1970s, my father was the general manager of a night club. He hired country and western bands on a weekly basis to perform for his customers. One day, my father decided to hold a fundraiser at his club, and he managed to get several bands to donate their profits to Perkins. Before my father presented Mr. Smith with the check, he wanted to make it clear that all proceeds from his fundraiser would be for the children of Perkins, and not for Perkins itself. He didn't want any of the money to cover administrative costs, because he felt that the kids needed it more to help with their studies.

One Friday afternoon, I was summoned to Mr. Smith's office, where my father had just arrived with the check in his hand. He wanted to give the money to Mr. Smith before he took me home for the weekend, but he also wanted me to be with him during the presentation. I remember how my father explained to Mr. Smith that every penny was to go to the children of Perkins. Mr. Smith was overwhelmed with surprise, but very grateful to my father for convincing several country and western bands to donate their time in order to help the children of Perkins.

Chapter 15

The High School Curriculum

Given all the influences that contributed to Perkins becoming less of an academic school, and where Chapter 766 didn't do me any good, I was fortunate to finish out my high school years at Perkins, taking the necessary courses that I needed in order to go to college. I admit that I complained a lot about some of the rules we had to follow, especially in the earlier years, but the one thing I've always said about my education at Perkins was that it was a quality education. I really believe that I learned as much as a sighted person learns in public school. After all, all of the school books at Perkins were either in print or Braille, depending on our individual needs, so I had no problem finding accessible material on any subject.

Usually it was the teacher who recommended and provided the books, but occasionally we'd have to go to the library to expand our knowledge. On rare occasions, especially when we had to do our Junior and Senior essays, we had to go off campus to a library that had the information we needed. This meant that we required a reader to work with us when we couldn't read the material. Usually, it was the Perkins social director who recruited readers to come onto the campus in the evenings, and it was up to us to request them. For the most part, these readers came from local colleges.

As most of you know, math is one of those love/hate subjects. If you're a math geek, or someone who just loves crunching numbers, then you love it. If you don't have the patience for numbers, fractions, algebra, or any other mathematical analysis, then it probably terrifies you, because it's not in your mindset. I am always fascinated by math on many levels. I enjoy good number tricks and the ability to analyze different problems relating to different branches of math. At Perkins, I took algebra, geometry, and trigonometry. Though the second year of algebra and the one year of trigonometry were optional, I took them anyway. For those of you who don't know what trigonometry is, it's the branch of math dealing with the relation of the sides and angles of triangles and of methods of deducing from given parts other required parts.

Before I talk about the advanced math, I'd like to begin by acknowledging Mrs. Stackhouse again, who I feel was one of the best teachers in the entire school, let alone math. For several years before I had her for a teacher, I learned a lot about fractions and understood them very well. However, nobody else defined a fraction the way Mrs. Stackhouse did. So, if anyone wants to know what a fraction is, I will simply tell you that a fraction is a division problem. That's how Mrs. Stackhouse defines it, and to me, that's the best definition there is.

My algebra class in my Freshman year of high school was similar to the movie *To Sir with Love*. As I tell the story, and if you're familiar with the movie, you'll understand what I mean.

Our regular teacher, Miss Uxbridge, was a great teacher and taught us well. She was also the last teacher who ever taught Latin at Perkins before it was dropped as a foreign language option.

In the middle of October, we learned that Miss Uxbridge

had to take an extended medical leave from school. Before she left, she introduced us to our temporary algebra teacher, who was a trainee from Africa. His name was Mr. B. It was immediately obvious that we were going to have a communication problem with this gentleman. He had a thick African accent and had trouble pronouncing some of our names. Though our grades did not suffer, and though we kept up with our work, it was difficult to grasp some of what he was telling us in the classroom. He knew how we felt, and he was embarrassed. As the weeks went by, we grew accustomed to Mr. B. and his ways, though the communication barrier was still there.

By the middle of May, Miss Uxbridge was ready to return as our teacher, which meant the end of our lessons with Mr. B. It was a Friday afternoon, Mr. B's last day. I arrived at class on time, and I believe my friend Juan did as well. The minutes were ticking away while we were waiting for the girls in our class to show up. We were a bit concerned, but we waited as long as we could. Suddenly, the door to the classroom opened, and the girls walked in carrying a large cake. They showed it to Mr. B. and yelled "Surprise!" Mr. B. was in total shock, and was at a loss for words as Jennie read the note out loud. I don't remember exactly what it said, but the cake was a gesture of appreciation to Mr. B. for putting up with us for nearly the entire school year. And, despite the communication barrier, he had tried his best and would be missed.

In my Sophomore year, I took geometry. Aside from the fact that I understood all of the logical postulates and axioms, and was able to prove most of the geometric theorems that we needed to prove, we actually had four days of geometry class every week instead of five. On the fifth day, our teacher let us play cards for the entire period as long as we had turned in our homework from the previous night. Usually, we played whist, which is a game involving four players in two partnerships.

There were only four kids in the class, so whist seemed like the appropriate card game to play while our teacher watched, commented, and advised.

I opted to continue with math in my Junior and Senior years, though I didn't have to. The second level of algebra was fun, despite a lot of opposing opinions, and trigonometry was challenging but tolerable, as long as you understood advanced formulas and why they work. Even though I don't apply my knowledge of trigonometry in everyday life, I was caught up in it when I learned it. I don't think too many people, while sipping their morning coffee, wonder how to figure out the sine or cotangent of angles inside their washer and dryer when doing laundry.

High school English class was traditional, and most of the work was not surprising. Aside from an occasional book report, we studied a lot about William Shakespeare and read such great novels as *Silas Marner* and *Great Expectations*. Some of the plays by Shakespeare that we read were the *Merchant of Venice*, *Romeo and Juliet*, *Hamlet* and *Julius Caesar*. Sometimes the class would be invited to the English teacher's apartment to listen to recordings of the plays so that we could have a better understanding of the Shakespearean dialect and dialog. We did lots of other reading as well, practiced some grammar, and took notes about many well–known authors.

In our Junior and Senior years, our biggest projects were major essays. We had to pick a topic, research it to the fullest, and write a complete essay, including an outline, footnotes, and a bibliography. I had to do most of my research off campus, where the libraries had no accessible reading material. As a result, the readers provided by the Perkins social coordinator assisted me, though I had to arrange the entire essay myself. I wrote about McCarthyism for my Junior essay, and my Senior essay was all about capital punishment, its history, and my thoughts on it.

I really can't talk about eighth–grade English that much, because it was uneventful except for three things: I received hundreds on most, if not all, of our spelling tests. The class read a goofy poem in chapel service called "The Courtship of the Yonghy–bonghy–bo," by Edward Lear. And on one occasion, the teacher asked me to read, but I thought she asked me to leave, so instinctively I got up and nearly left the room. That was an embarrassing moment, to say the least. I guess when you have a soft voice, the words read and leave can sound alike to your listeners.

After spending our seventh–grade year watching a gerbil family evolve in science class, we had science again as Freshmen, though it was a major subject then. This time around, we took care of our own individual plants instead of gerbils. We planted the seeds in pots of soil and watched as the leaves grew throughout the year. In Freshman science, we covered topics such as atoms, autumnal and vernal equinoxes, animal migration, air pressure, relative humidity, plant life, solids, liquids, gases, and how to test for granulated sugar.

Prior to my Sophomore year, I was often told by students who took biology that the worst part of the class was the dissection of frogs. If what the other kids said was true, then I was fortunate that frog dissection was not part of my biology class. We had a different teacher than most of the kids who took biology before me, so that may have been the difference. However, we did a number of fascinating things in biology, including learning about blood types. Once we learned about the various blood types and their RH factors, our teacher took a small sample of blood from each of us and actually told us what type we were. I thought that was extremely important, even though it was a scientific experiment, so I took the results quite literally.

Though Perkins only required two years of a foreign language, I took four years of Spanish. Prior to my Spanish education, I used to listen to my parents talk Portuguese to their friends, but could not really figure out what they were saying. After my Spanish training, I understood a lot of the Portuguese conversations because the two languages are closely related. My friend Pedro, who is a native Mexican, was happy I got to know his language, but when he was angry, he sometimes used Spanish words that we would never be taught. It's funny how the first words we normally learn of a foreign language are usually swear words or other dirty words. I had a couple of friends at Perkins who taught me some Italian curse words, even though I didn't know the first thing about the Italian language or their culture.

One of my favorite classes where I used my own creativity was computer class. In the 1970s, computers were built a lot differently than they are now. There were no laptops, flash drives, MP3 players, or hand-held smart phones. Most of the computer work was done on tapes that you would feed into a large machine with a built-in telephone, which acted as a dial-up feature. Most of your results were on paper, either in print or Braille, so that we really couldn't do much word processing. As you can imagine, a lot of computer tape and paper were wasted because everyone makes mistakes. We learned how to program the computer in the BASIC language. We programmed the computer to find Armstrong numbers, perform prime factorization of a given number, do logarithms and various math tricks, and play such games as Battleship and chess. I was so fascinated with how the computer did many tasks in BASIC that I had it do things that the teacher never knew about.

One day I set up a computer program where four contestants would guess a random number between one and four. Whoever guessed the number correctly would receive one point, and the computer would keep an accurate score until someone reached his goal of five or 10 points, depending on how I set up the program. I created a program which made the computer sound like an old-fashioned cash register, which rang between intervals of random length, as if a human was using the register. I also had the computer converse with me by printing out the answers. I would input the questions, and each question had its own answer, just as today's interactive toys work by the sound of your voice. Computer was a two-year course which most Juniors and Seniors took in the college preparatory division.

An optional academic course which was offered every two years, and which brought Juniors and Seniors together in the same class, was physics. Given that I had strong math and logical skills, plus a fascination with science, I decided to take the course. We learned about such things as specific gravity, centripetal force, centrifugal force, Newton's laws of motion, atomic physics, work, power, energy, and the coefficient of friction. One of the most interesting physics experiments that we did was to determine our own power. Each of us was asked to lift a two-kilogram weight one meter high as many times per minute as we could. My personal power was 14.3 watts, the weakest in the class. The strongest student had a power of 29 watts, based on this same experiment.

In our Freshman year, we took physiology, which included the study of the bones and muscles of the human body, along with how the human skeleton is arranged. We learned each muscle, its origin, its insertion, and its function. For example, the biceps muscle originates in the shoulder girdle, inserts at the radius bone, and performs flexion of the elbow.

As was the case with typing, I had learned all the state capitals before I attended Perkins. This knowledge came in handy during eighth-grade social studies. Though my grade in the class wasn't that bad, it wasn't as high as I would have liked. So, when our social studies teacher spent a couple of weeks on state capitals, the series of perfect test scores I received on this topic boosted my overall grade to a point I was satisfied with.

It wasn't until our Junior year that we visited the subject of American government once again. We took a year of U.S. history, a required academic subject. We covered everything from the House of Burgesses to the Boston Tea Party, and such famous historical figures as John Rolph, William Pitt, and Roger Williams. As a history class, we also went on a number of field trips, which I will describe later in more detail. For now, I will mention that we toured Plymouth Plantation, the Freedom Trail, Mystic Seaport, and Old Sturbridge Village. In fact, the Freedom Trail covered so much separate territory that we had to go twice.

Like most school children, we had our achievement tests, Junior SAT's (Scholastic Aptitude Tests) and Senior SAT's. Before I had the chance to learn much about why students had to take these tests, and how they might have proven to be controversial at times, I figured out rather quickly that not all high schools were on the same page scholastically. The SAT's were national tests, and several of the questions on the test referred to topics I had never studied. With that said, I passed the tests, which helped me qualify for college.

I mentioned earlier how some of us had work experience as part of our school curriculum. In my case, I worked at the research library for a year. I was paid by WGBH Television as part of a contract between Perkins and the station to transcribe interview programs which were on tape and put them into a typed format for the general public. The job for WGBH occurred in my second year of transcription class. In my first year, we learned how to use a Dictaphone, which was popular in the 1970s. The Dictaphone was a square machine, similar to a cassette player in many ways. But instead of using standard cassette or reel–to–reel tapes, which were the most popular recording media in those days, we used vinyl or plastic belts. The belt was oval in shape, and you inserted it into the Dictaphone in such a way that the belt would roll on a roller when the Dictaphone was turned on. Our lessons were recorded on the belt, and it was our job to insert the belt into the Dictaphone, play it, and type all the information that was recorded. If we needed to stop the recording in order to catch up, we used a foot pedal which controlled the Dictaphone by pausing, playing, and going back. The foot pedal made it easy for us to keep our hands off the Dictaphone and on the typewriter, where they should always be during a transcription project.

As part of our transcription training, we learned lots of legal terminology in case some of us wanted to pursue careers as legal secretaries. We used an electric typewriter throughout the class, and for some of us, it was our first time using one. I remember being fascinated by the automatic erase feature, which wasn't part of a manual typewriter. Of course we have computers today, with which you can correct mistakes to your heart's content without even using a piece of paper.

I also took a handwriting course at Perkins. While I learned how to write all 26 letters of the alphabet, I spent most of the time using a signature guide, which is designed so that the student won't write over his previous work. Aside from the signature guide, we were introduced to a check–writing guide, which allows a blind person to write his own checks. The check–writing guide, like the signature guide, is a template with long rectangular openings for you to write in. The template is placed over the piece of paper or check that you want to write on.

I previously talked about some of my courses in industrial arts, or shop, as some of us call it. I mentioned woodworking, caning, metal shop, and ceramics. There was another course known as home mechanics, which focused on different aspects of the home. The highlight of that class was the discussion of parallel versus series circuits. The teacher first demonstrated the parallel circuit by using wires and ordinary household light bulbs. When the project was complete, all four of the bulbs produced equal amounts of light. However, in a series circuit, the energy produced in the first light bulb was equally distributed among any additional bulbs added to the circuit, which made each working bulb dimmer as you added another one.

Cooking class was interesting, to say the least, and I always felt that we were scheduled at the wrong time of the day. Students got into the habit of eating what they cooked, so we often wondered if eating the food would affect our supper, especially when the class ran from 2:45 to 4:00 in the afternoon. We were also taught how to put out fires. We were told that if our oven mitts caught on fire while taking something out of the oven, we were to drop them on the floor and step on them. If our aprons caught fire, we were instructed to fall on the floor and continuously roll over until the fire was smothered and put out.

Chapter 16

Technology in the Seventies

When I speak of technology in this book, keep in mind that it was a lot different in the 1970s as opposed to what we have today. With that said, we were just as fascinated by changes in technology 40 years ago as we are today whenever something more progressive comes on the scene.

Prior to my time at Perkins, blind people had only two ways to read books. They either used their fingers to read Braille books, or someone else had to be their eyes or fingers and read the books to them. While most of us learned how to read Braille the same way, using both index fingers, we were taught two basic ways to write Braille. We either learned with the standard Braille writing machine, known as the Perkins brailler, or we used the slate and stylus.

I would say that 90% of Braille users prefer the Braille machine over the slate and stylus. Though the slate and stylus are convenient, in that you can put them in your pocket and take notes while traveling, you almost have to feel as though you are writing in reverse. The slate consists of four lines of Braille cells. It has two arms, which you close on a piece of paper. After the paper is locked in place, using the stylus, you punch the holes in each Braille cell that you want in order to form letters or words. This method of Braille writing is not the best, and it proved to be extremely frustrating, because many of us missed the exact holes we needed to punch. In fact, when I went for my certification test in 1997 in order to become a Braille teacher, despite the fact that I had over 30 years of Braille reading and writing experience at the time of the test, I failed it, because I had to demonstrate the slate and stylus as part of the exam.

Prior to 1970, totally blind people had only two ways to do complex math problems. They either wrote down all the formulas and steps in Braille, and then worked out the problems on paper the way a sighted person did with a pencil, or they used the abacus. Before I went to Perkins, I had never heard of the abacus, but when I used it in Lower School, I realized what a necessary tool it was at the time. Today, it isn't so necessary. But remember, I am putting myself in the world we lived in 40 years ago.

The abacus is an instrument for making calculations by sliding counters along rods or grooves. Each rod represents a place in the decimal system, whether it be the tens, hundreds, thousands, etc., or tenths, hundredths, or thousandths. Along with the 13 rods situated on the abacus, there is a long bar stretched across the rods. Positioned on the rod above the bar is one counter, or bead, while there are four counters, or beads, situated along each rod below the bar. When doing addition, you slide each lower bead up the rod until it hits the bar or another bead. When all four beads are moved, you have the number four. The bead situated above the bar represents the number five, and that bead has to be positioned against the bar.

To help make the process of addition simple, the inventor of the abacus developed some clever techniques, which are known as secrets. For example, if you want to add four plus four, the way to add four would be, "Set five, clear one." This means you move the bead which is above the bar, the number five bead, downward, and then move one of the other four beads down in order to clear it. There are other secrets for doing more complex addition and subtraction.

In the 1970s, talking scales were not popular, yet, so we used Braille scales to weigh ourselves in the cottages. For those of you who have never seen a Braille scale, you're probably wondering how we could read our weight in Braille if we had to bend down, causing our weight to be affected. But the scale wasn't built with that in mind. You stood upright on the scale, and there was a tall post situated in front of you with a Braille dial placed on top. As your weight was being recorded, the needle on the dial would move until it settled on a figure. We would feel where the needle was on the Braille dial, and then we'd know our weight.

Many of the kids at Perkins loved to play basketball. Although some of us played on the outdoor athletic field, and did very well at it, it was easier for someone with little or no vision to play basketball in the gym. Located near or at the rim of the basket was a metronome which gave a ticking sound, so that the players would know where the basket was at all times. Though Perkins never formed a basketball league, the way it did with baseball, basketball was a popular and competitive sport. Students would play one on one, and there were even games where the staff played against the students.

Earlier, I spoke briefly about the computer, and how I used it in class. At the time, we were fascinated by the prospect of using a computer, although today I think we'd all frown on it, given the types of computers we use now. The Perkins computer in 1971 had three parts: a keyboard with a paper feed, a box with the telephone and tape feed, and the storage area for Braille paper to be placed in such a way that it would be rolled out while the computer was printing. When you put all three of these computer components side by side, they would add up to the size of an average desk. There was no monitor or word processing. Every action we took on the computer was documented on hard copy, either in print or Braille, and every program we used or created had to be on a spool of tape, which was stored in a large box. There were no speech programs or spell check features, so if we made a mistake, we had to do it all over again and waste paper in the process. I have never seen wastebaskets fill up as fast as they did in computer class.

In the present, we use Google in order to look up any topic we want, instead of using an old–fashioned encyclopedia. But when I attended Perkins, there was no such thing as Google or any other search engine to make studying easier. In order to look up a specific topic, those of us who couldn't read print had to depend on an encyclopedia with a total of 140 Braille volumes. The complete set took up an entire back wall of the study hall, on several shelves. Even the Webster dictionary consisted of 72 Braille volumes. We've come a long way, Baby.

In the 1970s, most blind people I knew owned Braille watches. There was no such thing as a talking watch at the time, so unless you had usable sight, the Braille watch was acceptable, even though I'm not a fan of it. I never owned a Braille watch, but I've seen them. A blind person opens the cover on the watch face, allowing him to feel the hour and minute hands. The problem with this is that you run the risk of affecting the time if you touch the moving hands. Though the talking watch is extremely popular today, a lot of blind people still depend on their old–fashioned Braille timepieces because those particular watches don't disturb anybody else who might be in the vicinity. With that said, the talking watch is much more accurate, and you don't have to put your fingers under the lid, where you might affect moving parts.

To go along with those of us who wore watches, Perkins had its own method of telling time and informing us when to do certain things throughout the day. At 6:30 every morning, most of us were awakened by a school bell, which was heard in most of the cottages. For most of us, that was probably the worst sound of the day, as we had to wake up out of a sound sleep. Sometimes another bell would ring at 7:00, in case the cottage staff decided that 7:00 was breakfast time. During our school day, a bell would ring to end a period, while another rang to begin a new one. There were five minutes between classes, but we had two 10-minute breaks, one in the morning and one in the afternoon. During these 10-minute breaks, a bell would ring five minutes before the break ended, letting you know that it was time to get ready for the next class.

On top of the Howe Building, and visible for miles, was the famous Perkins tower. Inside the tower was a set of chimes, similar to those rung at Westminster Abbey. At 15-minute intervals, between 7:00 in the morning and 10:00 at night, the chimes would ring, giving us an indication of what time it was. At Christmastime, students were trained to play carols by using the chimes.

One of the most fascinating devices I came upon at Perkins accommodated a girl who was deaf and blind. This gadget helped her with mobility. When she approached an object, a beeping sound would go off, and where she had difficulty hearing, I can only assume it vibrated as well. There were many students at Perkins who had hearing as well as visual difficulties, and although most had usable vision, there were one or two who could neither hear nor see. One of my deaf-blind friends who had some usable vision decided to accommodate himself in his own bedroom. He invented a system which notified him when someone opened his bedroom door. A light would turn on, informing him that he had a visitor.

I mentioned how the Optacon was the first form of adaptive technology which allowed the blind to read print. One hand was placed over a set of vibrating pins while the other moved the small camera across written material, causing combinations of pins to vibrate in the shape of the letters that you moved the camera over. Given that some printed material was larger than others, the Optacon had a zoom adjustment to accommodate each situation. I recall reading the phone book with the Optacon, and though it wasn't easy, I knew that the process served to help us gain more independence. As is the case today, adaptive technology products such as the Optacon cost hundreds of dollars, so if a blind student wanted to buy one, he would have to dip into a large portion of his monthly check or any savings he might have. But students who were deaf and blind benefited greatly from using the Optacon, because of the vibrating images created when the camera scanned letters and words.

In 1976, the day came which marked the beginning of the reading technology we have today. I wasn't sure of what I'd be working with, but I was chosen as one of the first 10 blind students to evaluate a brand-new reading machine, put out by Kurzweil. The Kurzweil reading machine scanned printed material and converted it into speech. The manufacturers asked us to study the machine thoroughly so that we could come up with recommendations on how to improve it.

I remember visiting the manufacturing company in Cambridge, where I was introduced to the Kurzweil machine. As I describe this brand-new reader, which we all take for granted today, keep in mind that it was the first of its kind. It's been upgraded and simplified on numerous occasions over the years, while rival manufacturers have competed with Kurzweil to come up with similar reading machines.

The Kurzweil machine had three individual parts: the scanner, the keyboard, and the speakers. The scanner was at least three feet long and two feet wide. It was a large wooden case with a lid on top. In order to scan a page in a book, you would open up the book to the page you wanted to read, lift the lid, and place the page face-down on the glassy surface so that part of the book was on top of the glass while the other part was hanging off the side of the machine. Then you would close the lid, activate the moving part under the glass, and wait for the voice to read what was on the page. In those days, it took a long time for the machine to gather the information before it was read out loud. In 1976, the voice on a reading machine was foreign in sound, but understandable. We didn't really care how foreign it may have sounded; we were just so fascinated by this brand–new concept, which ultimately opened many doors for the blind.

As the Kurzweil machine started reading a page of print for me, I used the keyboard to pause, play, spell words, move up a line, down a line, or maneuver from word to word. I also learned to adjust the contrast between the printed material and the color of the page, as I realized that the machine read some of the printed material better than other parts. There was a bright light inside the machine which helped the movable scanner recognize the letters.

After I and nine other Perkins students gave the manufacturers our opinion of the Kurzweil machine, the manufacturers tried their best to make the necessary improvements. Eventually, a second type of Kurzweil machine was sent to Perkins, and it was used for a new course which was added to the school curriculum. I used to read newspaper articles, typed documents, and other necessary items, all the while knowing that the machine wasn't perfect. Today, I have a much smaller and more compact reading machine in my home, one which you can actually carry around with you if you feel like it, even though it's a desktop model.

Chapter 17

The Darker Side of Perkins

As most blind people know, we try our best to prove to ourselves and to society that we can compete on equal terms with the sighted. We do this because we know we are capable of living independently, holding down a job, taking care of a family, paying the bills, traveling alone, and getting a quality education. Throughout our lives, it sometimes feels like an uphill battle convincing the general public of what we, the blind, can do. On the other hand, other blind people are taking it a step further, whether they know it or not. When they try to prove how they can compete on equal terms with the sighted, they also prove how to get in trouble, just as some sighted criminals and daredevils can. Yes, there are blind people who pull stunts and commit crimes, too.

During my eight years at Perkins, I heard it all. I'll start by talking about the simple stunts, such as shortsheeting a bed or putting shaving cream on the sheets in order to aggravate somebody. When a bully knows that he's making someone angry, he feeds off it and develops a sociopathic personality toward the victim. The bully doesn't care that he may get caught pulling a stunt. He'll continue to do it as long as he gets a rise out of the victim, because that's stimulating for the bully.

More often than not, the victim didn't know who was playing tricks, because the bully was too clever to let the victim find out. When I discovered those filthy Braille letters in my study hall cubicle, I was able to figure out who wrote them because, at the time, I was having problems with those particular kids. This was the exception to the victim/bully rule.

At Perkins, there were bullies, and then there were daredevils. Several boys, despite their vision loss, learned how to pull the fire alarm successfully, causing massive chaos in the cottage or in the school building. Obviously these boys didn't care about the consequences, except for the fact that they received attention, whether it was positive or negative. Another boy, who obviously thought he was bored with life, decided to do something about it. He urinated into a wall socket. I would say that his friends got a big charge out of that, but probably not the charge he got. While on the subject of urinating, someone did it in a cup and then told his friend to drink it without telling him what it was. Oh, and how can we discuss determination without talking about sex? Though I wasn't in Potter Cottage at the time, I learned that two boys, ages 10 and 11, snuck out of the cottage at midnight, snuck into Glover, and had sex with two of the girls in their bedrooms without getting caught. So here's a word to the wise. Never underestimate the blind.

Though several students were either suspended or expelled from Perkins for committing unlawful acts, some behavior appeared to be overlooked. Albert was one of my best friends in both the Lower and Upper School, and though he had a vivid imagination and a certain degree of intellect, he was bullied constantly by those who recognized a flaw in him that they thrived on. What the bullies did not bargain for was Albert's temper. One day, Albert reached his breaking point and threw a Braille machine at someone's head. If the intended victim had not had some sight, he would most likely not have been aware of the heavy Braille machine flying in his direction, something that might have killed him. Yet it seemed that the event was overlooked.

I know one thing. If I had been the intended victim, whether I had bullied Albert or not, I would have at least told someone in authority what was done. Ask yourself these questions. Would you have been able to justify Albert's throwing a Braille machine at someone's head as retaliation for bullying? Would you have written the incident off as an act by someone with severe anger issues and emotional problems? Or would you have treated Albert as a common criminal by punishing him for trying to severely injure or kill somebody? No matter what answer you might give, I feel the matter should have been looked into further.

To prove my point, I can tell you that this wasn't the only time Albert used his anger in a very dangerous fashion. One day, in an attempt to get even with a bully, Albert used his head as a weapon and bashed it against a boy's chest. Well, the boy happened to be me. Albert was so angry that he didn't realize he was bashing me instead of the bully. In cooking class, once, someone bullied Albert so badly that he chased after the boy with a kitchen knife. I wasn't there, but according to sources, all that was done about the incident was that the teacher told Albert to calm down and put the knife away. On another occasion, while Albert was walking down the Howe Building corridor, several students were viciously teasing him. In his haste to get even, Albert swung his arms and hit an innocent girl who was walking by.

Though Perkins is a private school which was thought of as an institution, it wasn't without its drug addicts, alcoholics, and thieves. Some would think that we were cared for, monitored, and coddled so much that we wouldn't even know how to smuggle booze and drugs onto the campus. Well, when we were given an opportunity to travel independently, some kids managed to learn how to do the unthinkable.

My friend Sandra, who recently passed away at a young age, was a very bright student with a lot of promise. She had a sense of humor and liked all of us, but she had a weakness for alcohol. On one occasion she got into trouble for drinking at Watertown Square, and on other occasions she drank on the school grounds and was suspended at least once.

We can always agree how wrong it is for teenagers to drink, whether they are in a private school, a public school, or at home, but it doesn't help matters when authority figures, who are supposed to set a good example, do the same thing. It's been alleged that several faculty members at Perkins drank privately, and one of the counselors kept a bottle of brandy in his desk drawer that a student caught him with. This is not an attack on the school itself, because we can't hold the school responsible for every wrongdoing that goes on. The faculty members I referred to are now either retired or deceased. I am positive that if the administration had heard of any use of alcohol by the staff, immediate action would have been taken in order to put a stop to it.

Earlier in this book, I talked about the abuse that some of us took from two of the lower school housemothers. If this had happened today, these women would have been fired, taken to court, or both, because society is more reactive now than it was 40 years ago.

The only way I would hold Perkins or any other school responsible for wrongdoings by its staff or students is if the school knew about them and did nothing. I am convinced that the Perkins administration did everything humanly possible to stop unpleasant behavior that they were aware of, because they had no problem suspending or expelling kids for drugs, theft, drinking, or any other offense.

In 1975, a nice young man named Ron arrived at Perkins from New Jersey as a high school student. He was likable, cheerful, and smart. What we didn't know at the time was that he was a heroin addict. One evening, someone found Ron passed out on one of the Perkins parking lots. It was later revealed that he had overdosed on heroin, and shortly after that, he was no longer part of the student body. The incident rocked Perkins so badly that our cottage housemaster kept us after supper one night to talk about the consequences of taking drugs, and he said that what had happened to Ron should be a very important lesson for all of us.

While we acknowledged what the housemaster said, drug activity did not stop. In 1976, another known drug addict appeared on the scene, and soon we heard that Perkins was conducting a major investigation on the campus in order to find out how much drug activity was really going on. During this investigation, several of us were questioned by the staff about what we were doing and whom we were spending time with.

My friend Jane happened to fall in love with this drug addict, and despite warnings from her friends about the potential danger of such a relationship, she refused to listen. One day, Jane disappeared from Perkins, never to be heard from again, and we all assumed that it had something to do with the drug addict. We were all shocked and saddened by the situation, especially Jane's English teacher. Jane was halfway through her Senior year when this happened, and her English grade was the best ever. The teacher blamed Jane's disappearance on the drug addict, and said he would hang the guy on a wall the next time he saw him. I don't know what happened to the drug addict, because I never saw him on the Perkins campus again. I think he was smart enough to realize that at least half the student body would either blame him or try to go after him, because we believed he had caused Jane to run away. Now, however, Jane is doing quite well. She settled down, got married, and had several children.

Mr. Smith, the director of Perkins, was fully aware that

many of the students were misbehaving in one way or another. He, as well as the Upper School principal, had a hand in some of the suspensions and expulsions, and most likely grew tired of it all. I guess you could say that Mr. Smith nearly reached his breaking point one day when it was announced that he wanted the entire Upper School student body to meet with him in the chapel after school. I had no idea why everyone had to meet with him, and many of us were jumping to all sorts of conclusions. What the heck had we all done wrong? We knew that some kids were behaving badly, but not the entire Upper School!

At 4:15 that afternoon, we all gathered in the chapel, anxiously waiting to find out why it was so important for the director of Perkins to talk to us. When we found out, I remember thinking how we were all teenagers, and that the treatment by the director was a bit over the top. The reason why the entire Upper School student body was summoned to the chapel that day was so that Mr. Smith could lecture all of us about swearing. Apparently, he had heard that there was an excessive amount of swearing on campus, so he felt he had to remind all of us about how the use of foul language was totally and completely inappropriate. I agreed with him. However, I questioned his tactics. While it was true that many of the students cursed on a regular basis without caring who heard them, many of us never swore, and we felt we shouldn't have been dragged to a childish meeting if we already knew better.

Halloweens at Perkins were as festive as they could have been under the circumstances. Obviously, it was tough for the kids to make the rounds for candy while they were figuratively confined to the campus. With that said, the staff in each cottage made additional fruit and candy available to the residents. On one occasion, a sharp object was found inside an apple. I was told that it was either a needle or a razor blade. The staff called attention to it and made sure no one had access to the apple. As for who did the dirty deed, I don't know, but I hope that if the person was caught, he was reprimanded to the fullest.

To prove how times have changed, and how potential lawsuits, ones that would be filed now, never were in the 1970s, I would like to talk about an incident that fortunately never happened to me, but which happened to one of my best friends, who left Perkins shortly thereafter.

As I mentioned earlier, Lower School kids were required to take swimming lessons as part of their curriculum. The key word in that statement is "required." I'm sure that some kids tried to get out of swimming for a number of reasons, especially for fear of the water, but they were fighting a losing battle.

The boy I'm going to talk about was a tough, fearless dude who takes chances to this day. In fact, he was one of the kids who snuck into Glover to have sex at midnight with a 12–year–old girl. For the purpose of this discussion, I'll call him Ralph. In 1972, Ralph was in Lower School, and like all other kids in his age bracket, he had to take swimming lessons. One day while he was in the pool, the swimming instructor didn't like what she observed. Perhaps she didn't like how Ralph was swimming, or perhaps Ralph took sick, or maybe it was something else. To me, her solution to the problem was absolutely disgusting, to say the least. She decided to hold Ralph's head under water for a period of time. First of all, if my head was held under the water against my will by a swimming instructor, I'd waste no time reporting her to the principal, the director, my parents, and anyone else who would listen. Not only would I hope she got fired, but I'd see to it that she never taught swimming again.

Ralph was a tough, confident, cocky kid, but the end result was probably not what he expected. He reported the swimming teacher to his parents, and they took him out of swimming for good. The instructor continued to teach swimming and physical education for years to come. Now you would think that Ralph would remain in swimming class while the instructor was relieved of her duties. No. She remained, and he was excused for the rest of the year.

This is one more example of society 40 years ago. It's probably why students didn't want to report their teachers to the principal if they felt their teachers had done something foolish or wrong. We may have simply believed that no one would listen to us, so that's why we allowed stupid stuff to happen, like when Mr. Mills made us eat empty hot dog buns because one classmate disagreed with everyone else about what should go on the hot dogs. I know that an empty bun and a near drowning are at opposite ends of the maltreatment spectrum, but my point is that in both cases, the teachers were never reprimanded. We were intimidated by Mr. Mills and regarded him as our superior, no matter how unreasonable he was about the hot dogs. Given that Ralph had only a few months left at Perkins before transferring to a public school, he and his parents probably thought that the best solution was to get him away from the mean swimming teacher instead of having her fired. With that said, his parents may have tried to have her fired, but we're talking about 1972, not 2012. Today, when society is more reactive, the swimming instructor, the two abusive housemothers, and Mr. Mills would most likely lose their jobs.

I have commented many times about how we live in a sue-happy society, but any lawsuit filed today against those teachers and housemothers would have my full support. Any housemother who threatened to execute one of her boys for not eating his supper should be put in jail for a long time. By the way, Miss Jones, the tough housemother from Potter Cottage, banged a boy's head against the wall and was supposedly fired. However, she returned to Perkins a few years later and lived in one of the cottages with her husband, my geometry teacher. If I had been Mr. Smith, the director, I would not have allowed Miss Jones back on the campus, no matter whose wife she was. I wouldn't want her to have any contact with the children after she had abused so many of them verbally and physically.

This chapter would not be complete if I didn't talk about the Perkins goon. This particular boy, who arrived on the scene in 1972 as a high school Freshman, was of average height and weight, but extremely muscular. He lived a very rough life back in his home state of New Jersey. He was very street smart, intelligent, and confident, but he didn't know how to channel his anger and aggression.

It didn't matter where I was. If the goon happened to be in my vicinity, he would try to pick a fight or get physical with me most of the time. In study hall, for example, he would corner me and give me a head lock, grab hold of my shoulders, pinch, or kick me. I tried to fight him off, but realized that it was a lost cause. Admittedly, I was a lot weaker than he was, so I don't know what was more embarrassing or shameful, his fighting with someone much weaker, or my allowing it to happen so often. He'd try to fight with me in chorus rehearsal, in the cottage, in the rec room, outside, and any other place that God created for mankind.

My whole problem was that I allowed the goon to get to me, and I reacted in a way that made him want to fight all the more. If I had simply toughened up and shown him that his dumb attempt at being a man didn't bother me, he might have stopped. It's that old story about victims versus bullies. He was definitely not a stupid kid. Whatever it was that played this part in his personality stemmed from an extremely traumatic childhood. I'm not sure if he ever had therapy, but based on what I know of him, it would not be a bad idea if he had some type of counseling even now.

Other students had similar problems with the goon, and it wasn't long before he was extremely unpopular with his peers, as well as the staff. Given that he had some degree of intelligence and common sense, there were times when he was cordial, but those times were few and far between. I regarded him as the chief bully. Yet he actually had a few friends, who, for the most part, tried to be like him or wanted to stoop to his level.

I reported the goon to the principal on several occasions and felt very comfortable ratting him out, because I knew that other kids did, as well, and that many of the staff members disliked him. Where the goon continued with his act on a regular basis, many of us knew that his days at Perkins were numbered, and we were right. It took two years, but eventually the goon was dealt with.

Today, he lives in Pennsylvania, and even though he is in his fifties instead of his teens, he still shows signs of his original personality. Even now, he occasionally pulls pranks and spreads false rumors about other people. If any of you know whom I'm talking about, it's best to either be a step ahead of him or simply avoid him.

Chapter 18

Beyond Blindness

From the time I first heard about Perkins School until my second or third year as a student there, I made one simple assumption: that the only problem that the students at Perkins had was their loss of vision. They couldn't see very well, or at all, and the local school systems couldn't help them anymore, so they ended up at Perkins.

Later on, I realized that there were different reasons why kids lost their vision. My friend Everett lost his at age nine because of a brain tumor, while many other kids were born blind, with a condition called RLF, which was a direct result of too much oxygen in the incubator. Some students had tunnel vision, while others were extremely farsighted but needed a magnifier to read large print books. The bottom line was that if you were a child with varying degrees of vision loss, Perkins was the answer for you.

Of course Miss Jones thought I was the only kid at Perkins with eyes like Superman, but that was her problem. She actually wanted to believe that I had allowed myself to be uprooted from my comfortable home and live 65 miles away at a school for the blind in order to fake a vision loss. I shed many a tear my first few weeks away from home, so if I had all of my sight, why couldn't I just stay home? If I had all of my sight, why would the state of Massachusetts tell my parents that I needed to go to Perkins at age 12? If I had all of my sight, then what the heck were the eye doctors thinking when they diagnosed the cause of my partial vision loss at a young age? I didn't know that a housemother would go to such lengths to attempt to prove that a student at a school for the blind wasn't blind at all. When she asked me to tell her the colors of the clothing that each boy in Potter Cottage was wearing, I should have been wise enough to ask her what color her judgment was –– that is, if she had any judgment at all.

As time went by, I realized that many of the kids had other issues, issues that never really came to the forefront, at least in my presence.

There were several boys who had brain tumors, and some of them passed away at a very young age. Everett lived for a long time. However, I learned several years ago that he died after he fulfilled his dream of meeting a major league baseball player. Given Everett's history of diabetes, I would say that it was the disease that won the battle for his life.

I'm not usually a person who supports political correctness, but occasionally I take issue with how people are labeled. When I was younger, I learned about retardation as it pertained to a person with mental challenges. But as I became an adult, I stopped using the term altogether. To me, the word "retarded" demeans the people we're referring to. Being that those who are labeled as retarded have special needs, I prefer to speak of these individuals as having such needs, or to say that they have developmental disabilities.

You may ask what this has to do with Perkins. Well, when I learned that several of the boys in Potter Cottage had problems hearing as well as seeing, I told people that I knew boys who were deaf and blind. The housemothers, however, used a term that struck a negative chord with me. They took the letter D for deaf, combined it with the letter B for blind, and referred to these boys as Dee Bees. Somehow the term "Dee Bee" takes the humanity away from what the boy really is, and makes him appear to be like something on a shelf. How would you react if I asked you what that Dee Bee was doing over there, or why that boy was picking on those Dee Bees? I'm blind, but I'm also slightly overweight, so maybe I should be called an O–Bee.

Many of the boys I lived with, especially in Lower School, had something that psychologists, social workers, teachers, and other professionals talk about on a regular basis. These boys, for the most part, had their intelligence, but they possessed quirks from earlier in their childhood which they had never outgrown. Some would clap their hands randomly, while others rocked, invented unusual fantasies, or watched television programs that most of us stop watching by age 10. How many 14–year–olds do you know who still watch *Sesame Street*? My friend George did, and loved it.

Sometimes the housemothers tried to put a stop to these bad habits, but they failed more than they succeeded. My friend Vic was a *Star Trek* fanatic. He talked about it day and night, and if you happened to be his roommate, he'd put you to sleep every night with "Red alert! Red alert!" Well, a housemother was fed up with it. One day, she was so tired of hearing about *Star Trek* that she told Vic to stop playing with the other kids for a whole hour and just sit on a bench quoting *Star Trek* phrases. Her hope was that the other boys would walk by the bench and hear him repeat *Star Trek* terms to himself, making him look foolish. Through her method of reverse psychology, the housemother felt that Vic would get the message and stop obsessing about that program.

Though many parents have no problem raising blind children, professionals believe that some do not discipline a blind child as much as a sighted child, and will subconsciously allow their blind child to continue doing things that sighted children outgrow at a very young age. Combined with this theory is the belief that a blind child may not realize what's wrong with his bad habit if he can't see his environment, especially when his parents are allowing the habit to continue. Given the fact that many parents handle their blind children quite well, I will only focus on parents who go from one extreme to the other. Some parents ignore the blind child, leaving him to his own devices, while others do the exact opposite and pamper him to the point where his life is negatively affected for a long time.

In school, I knew a blind boy whose mother scolded his little sister for not tying his shoes. Every weekend, it was the little girl's job to tie her brother's shoes on a regular basis, and when she forgot to do it one day, she was reprimanded. Instead of the mother punishing her sighted daughter, she should have used that same energy in teaching her blind son to tie his shoes. After all, he was 10 years old, and I don't care if you have vision or not; you should be able to tie your shoes at age 10.

I tied my shoes every day at Perkins, and if my shoelaces were too loose, Miss Tully would see to it that I tied them properly. But in the meantime, this other boy, who I'm sure was called on the carpet for the same reason, would go home and let his eight–year–old sister tie his shoes for him, at his mother's instruction.

This is where I really sympathize with the Perkins housemothers. They do their best to teach these kids what is and isn't appropriate, but when the kids go back home, it all gets ruined if the parents pamper, coddle, and spoil them rotten.

I have one more comment to make about the mother who asked her little girl to tie her blind brother's shoes. She led her daughter to believe that this is how it is for all blind children. Therefore, when the girl got older, she too may have pampered blind kids, because that's all she knew. This belief does not help the blind function independently in society. Although these parents do not intend to mislead or hurt anyone when they coddle their blind children, their own stereotypical beliefs are creating a discriminatory monster.

Before my friend Everett lost his sight at age nine, I believed he had a very normal childhood. When his vision was abruptly taken from him, his mother overprotected him so much that I don't believe he was allowed to face the reality of his blindness. I'm not a psychiatrist, but I witnessed many examples which support my belief. Everett had a lot of fear, and that fear dominated his life at Perkins. He was petrified of the water and tried every trick in the book to get out of swimming class on a regular basis. He even attempted to be excused from gym, especially if he knew we were going to do things he was terrified of, such as forward rolls, backward rolls, ladders, and balancing acts. He simply did not have any faith or trust in his own body, which I'm sure he had before he lost his vision.

Many of us have fears, but Everett's were extreme. Sometimes while we were sitting in the classroom, he would cry out, "My eyes are sinking in! My eyes are sinking in!" None of us really knew what that meant, but because he believed it, he was horrified. I feel that because he couldn't see, he imagined things that were happening to his eyes, and he was too defenseless to know better. Otherwise, why on Earth would he believe his eyes were sinking in?

The pathetic thing about this situation, other than Everett's behavior, is that once he left Perkins and went out into the sighted world, many people would think that this is how a blind person behaves. They would think that he is supposed to be scared of life, be afraid of challenge, not trust his own body, and cry when he gets scolded or has to take his insulin shot. But Everett is simply one blind individual with these types of fears, the same way that individual sighted people have problems. This does not mean that all blind people behave like Everett, or that all sighted people expect them to.

My friend Ralph also lost his sight at a young age, but he came from a progressive family that allowed him to be himself. While he adjusted to his blindness, he got tougher and became a real daredevil. He had sex with 12-year-olds, played football in public high school, did drugs and slept around while in college, learned valuable professions, and raised a family. Even though I don't agree with some of the things Ralph did when he was growing up, he was not pampered because he was blind. He was allowed to make his own judgments and learn from his mistakes when he made them. While he regrets some of what he did, he is an upstanding member of the community today. He can cook, raise children, repair complex machinery, perform disc jockey work, clean toilets, change diapers, fight the legal system, and be a passionate sports fan. But guess what? He's blind!

My friend Rita had a strong passion for the Boston Red Sox, and she probably still does. Whenever I saw her on the Perkins campus, most of our conversations were about the Red Sox, because I'm one of their biggest fans as well. What I didn't know was how Rita's passion for the Red Sox bordered on obsession. No matter what Rita did, or where she went, she needed to wear red socks. Though she couldn't see, she was satisfied when she was told that her socks were red. One morning, someone suggested that Rita change her dress during her lunch break, because she wasn't color coordinated. Rita was glad to do that, as long as her socks were red. By the way, Rita was in her teens at the time.

With the changes that Mr. Smith made during his time as director came a new awareness that the students and faculty had to acquire. As more special needs children arrived on the scene, many of us had to adjust to new behaviors and learn to cope with them. While most of these kids behaved normally, others had very severe emotional problems. They had unusual episodes of anger where they screamed and became violent. The bullies had a field day with this. In their mind, they had found more kids to pick on, and they didn't care what kind of mental problems these kids had.

Whenever a new kid joined the student body, it was as though the bullies would interview him to determine whether or not he was worth teasing. It wasn't necessarily about intelligence, because some of the students with special needs possessed it. It was more about quirks, habits, or lifestyles. But in some cases, it was about things the kids couldn't help. Children were picked on because of bad body odor, obesity, hyperactivity, and excessive rocking, but they were also teased about their names and nationalities.

My friend George, the boy who watched *Sesame Street* into his teens, was, and is, reasonably intelligent. However, when he was in Lower School, he clapped his hands randomly and made funny sounds. You may ask, What's wrong with that in Lower School? Well, fifth–graders don't normally do those things. As for George's habits, his family probably allowed them to continue because he was blind, so in the family's eyes, he was different. Many students knew George in both Lower and Upper School, and because some were familiar with his Lower School antics, such as clapping, making odd sounds, and watching *Sesame Street* at age 14, they picked on him later. George is of Polish heritage, so bullies would walk by him and use the slang term for a Polish person. George expressed his desire for them to knock it off, which simply made them do it all the more.

Though I've been using fake names in order to identify almost all of the students and staff, this next story is so delicate that I won't even mention the fake name I've already used for this boy. When the boy was in Upper School, he had to do what every other boy did: mop the bedroom floor when it was his turn. Some of his roommates realized that the boy didn't want to mop, so they started picking on him for it. First, they called him Mop, which caused him to have temper tantrums. Then they called him Closet. The tantrums got worse, but the other fellows wouldn't stop teasing him, because they seemed to enjoy driving him nuts.

At first, I believed that they called him Closet because of where the mop was kept, but I was very wrong! It's true that the term "Closet" bothered this kid as much as the term "Mop," but the closet held another delicate significance in his life which he was obviously ashamed of. According to several sources, this boy was caught performing homosexual acts in the closet with his roommate, and word spread. Normally, the Perkins grapevine was extremely ripe, but not ripe enough for me to find out until someone told me about this 25 years after I graduated.

Another sad state of affairs was when kids were ridiculed because of their weight. Two girls that I knew, one of whom was a classmate of mine, were two of the nicest girls you'd ever want to meet. But because they were overweight, they were constantly made fun of. Sometimes you don't have to eat a lot to gain weight, so we can't necessarily blame these girls for their condition. In regard to this issue, I'd like to make a personal observation. I don't know how any Perkins student could gain weight by eating the school's food. Our diet was rigid, and we didn't spend enough time in the rec room to pig out and gain the weight that some of these students possessed.

In 1974, I met a developmentally disabled boy from New Jersey named Chuck who had unusual talent. You may ask why he was considered developmentally disabled. To begin with, he was placed in the ungraded division scholastically, while he lived in a cottage with other undergraduate special needs children in the new program Mr. Smith had created. In spite of that, he possessed extraordinary skills. If Chuck smashed a transistor radio into pieces, he would put it back together and make it work again.

The first time I met him was during an after–school sports

activity, and he seemed to be a very likable boy. I knew he was developmentally disabled based on his demeanor. While we were in the boys' locker room after getting out of the swimming pool, something happened that triggered a very negative impulse in Chuck. He became extremely annoyed and frustrated, and suddenly, he let out a loud and continuous scream which resonated throughout the entire locker room and swimming area. As I found out later, Chuck's erratic and frightening behavior was quite frequent. If he knew he was late for class, or if he believed he was going to be late, Chuck would develop extreme aggression. He would run up and down the corridors while stamping his feet. With his violent temper, Chuck would yell foul language and shout at the top of his lungs, "I'm fired. I'm fired!"

He was so out of control, and made such a public display, that he disrupted nearly all the activities that took place in the Upper School, to the point where staff members had to stop what they were doing in order to restrain him. Chuck would run in many different directions, making it nearly impossible for anyone to stop the violence. All we would hear was, "I'm late, I'm fired! I'm late, I'm fired!" One day it got so bad that he had to be restrained by several students and staff in the rec room entrance, and I was told not to go inside. However, if people had enough patience, they would usually succeed in calming Chuck down after one of his episodes.

Chapter 19

Going Places

When we had the opportunity to get away from our routines, we usually looked forward to it. Perkins offered a number of ways for the student body to enjoy life, explore, and discover new horizons. Like any other child, I enjoyed some of the challenges, though I limited my participation. That's because most of what the students did took place on weekends, and I always preferred to go home then. Other students preferred to go home every weekend, too, but when there was a campus activity that they wanted to participate in, they stayed there over the weekend.

Sometimes, students who stayed at Perkins over the weekend took field trips off campus just for a change of scenery. One of the most common adventures involved maple syrup. I don't remember if the children went to New Hampshire or Vermont, but the syrup was made as part of science class. On the Perkins campus, kids tapped trees and then turned the sap into yummy maple syrup. I believe you had to get 40 gallons of sap for one gallon of syrup. The sap was then filtered in order to eliminate all the bark and debris. Once all the junk was filtered out, the sap was boiled. The students were each given one small jar of syrup to take home. On the field trip, students checked out the trees there and took a hands–on tour of the factory where the sap is filtered and boiled. They ate buckwheat pancakes with syrup for lunch and snow candy for dessert.

During the week, I had plenty of adventure, because teachers, housemothers, and other organizers made sure we ventured out, even during school time. The first field trip that I remember took place in my fifth–grade year. Mr. Mack took us to different parts of the campus in order to show us the blue collar side of the school. We visited Howe Press, which was regarded by many as the chief manufacturing company on campus. At Howe Press, some of the students checked out all the innards of a Braille machine and typed on the stereotyper, which produced Braille on thick metal plates that were used in a brailling press. Besides repairing braillers, Howe Press also sells them, along with Braille paper, slates, and styluses. They even publish many books in Braille, and they use the National Library Service to assist them. Many of us continue to depend on our braillers, even though technology is trying very hard to push the Braille machine out of our lives. No matter what's on the market today, I will always use my trusty brailler, which was probably manufactured at the Howe Press many years ago. There is nothing like it, especially where Braille is my world.

Singing Beach is a very nice recreation spot in Manchester, Massachusetts, on Cape Ann. I heard that the beach is named that because the sand sings as you walk on it. On June 9, 1970, and June 8, 1971, I went with the Lower School boys by bus to Singing Beach as part of Picnic Day. The Lower School girls went to an amusement park, while most of the Upper School attended the aforementioned Junior Fair on that particular day of the school calendar.

Several of the teacher trainees and Potter staff accompanied us while we spent a relaxing day at the beach. Many of us spent time in the water, swimming and jumping the waves. After lunch, we were told to wait a half hour before returning to the water so that our food would be digested properly. I'm sure that many of the boys had no problem swimming in the cool water at Singing Beach because of their extensive training in swimming class. At that time, I was learning the main highways of the Greater Boston area, so as the bus was traveling to and from Singing Beach, I discovered that Route 128 continued north from Watertown up toward Gloucester, which is on the tip of Cape Ann.

One afternoon during my sixth–grade year, Mr. Mills decided to take the class horseback riding. It was a lot of fun, and quite relaxing. It's one thing for a horse to guide you while you're on its back, but it's another to be part of a tandem on a bicycle. On and off campus, it was quite common for a student with vision to ride in tandem with a student with no vision. The student with the most vision would sit on the front bicycle seat, while the one with the least amount of vision sat in the seat behind him. A tandem bike is built with two seats, and both parties participate in the pedaling.

In public school, students are required to attend classes 180 days a year, although that rule seems to be bent more often than I care to admit. However, let's assume that you had to go to school for 180 days each year. Did any of your teachers ever take you on a field trip which disrupted the plans that other teachers had for you on that day? Earlier in this book, I brought up the subject of how Perkins teachers might have felt when another teacher took their class on an outing which lasted an entire school day.

Allow me to put this more into perspective now. If my history teacher wanted to take his class away from the Perkins campus for several hours, did he consult my English teacher, my Spanish teacher, my math teacher, and my gym teacher? Keep in mind that these other teachers had probably prepared lessons for us on the day of our field trip, and they didn't know what our history teacher had in mind. I'm not sure if we were required to go to school for 180 days a year at Perkins, but I knew that whenever our class took a field trip, we didn't go to school at all that day, and we never made the missed classes up. So, with that said, where do we draw the line about required school days? I wonder now if there was a huge power struggle going on between the teacher who took us off campus and those who were affected by our absences. I wonder if the school principal stepped in and set the boundaries for each side. I know that our chorus teacher had no problem preempting our regular academic classes when it came to Christmas concert rehearsals. He made sure we had those rehearsals during school time, as well as in the evening.

When I was a teenager, it didn't matter to me how other teachers might have felt when one of them took us off campus. It didn't occur to me that we shouldn't be skipping school, or that the other teachers should be upset because the field trip affected their lesson plans for us. When I arrived in Upper School, field trips off campus were quite common, and they proved to be extremely educational. Unlike the previous one-week trip to the Cape Cod National Seashore, which became an annual tradition at Perkins for decades, each of my remaining field trips only lasted half a day or one entire day.

In my seventh-grade year, our class visited a big textile mill in Andover. We learned how the workers manufactured various types of textiles and how those were put to good use. During that same year, we took a trip to the *Boston Globe* in order to understand how a major newspaper is run. We listened to the sounds of all the printing presses and took a quick tour of the most important areas of the workplace. Keep in mind that 40 years ago, there was no Internet, so the entire operation of the *Boston Globe*, as well as any other newspaper at the time, revolved around hard copy and actual newsprint. In eighth grade we visited the Somerville, Massachusetts courthouse and sat in on a few court proceedings in order to learn more about the judicial system, which was a topic in social studies.

The Boston Museum of Science was another interesting place, especially given that I've always enjoyed science. I was particularly impressed with the exercise bike that lit up a few lights. As you moved the pedals on the bike faster and faster, lights would go on, starting with the one at the bottom. Our goal was to light up all four of them, which made us extremely proud to be excellent bike riders. As I talked on the makeshift telephone, I heard my words come back to me. In the 1970s, many of the exhibits at the science museum weren't what they are now, for obvious reasons, but nevertheless, if you are a science buff, it shouldn't matter what era you live in, because something will always fascinate you.

Once in a while, whenever there was a good Broadway play or a movie to see on or off campus, groups of us would attend. I remember our English teacher, Mr. Acres, taking us to see *Gone with the Wind* and *Great Expectations*. The North Building on the Perkins campus had a movie theater, so arrangements were easy. *Great Expectations* was one of my favorite novels that we read in English class, even though it had two separate endings, depending on which version you read. We also spent an evening at the Schubert Theater in Boston watching a performance of the original musical *Grease*. No, it wasn't the version with John Travolta. It was two years more before that version was produced.

In my Junior year, 1975–1976, when our history teacher took us on field trips, it always seemed as though they were more adventurous than we had expected. We went in all kinds of weather, took various modes of transportation, and on one occasion two of us nearly got lost.

I will now describe our exciting and fearless adventures on these trips.

In the fall of 1975, my history class, accompanied by

another class, spent an afternoon at the Plymouth Plantation. Before we went, I had no knowledge of what took place over there and how much of a learning experience it was. After I went, I recommended the experience to anyone who was curious to learn exactly how the Pilgrims lived in the 17th century.

When you arrive at the Plymouth Plantation, you are no longer living in the present. As you walk from building to building, you meet actors who make believe they are the Pilgrims. If you try to talk to them about what's going on now, they won't understand what you mean. For example, don't talk about radio, electricity, or television, because they won't know what you're talking about. When you are at Plymouth Plantation, you are living in the Pilgrims' world, and they will gladly explain it to you as if they are your friends. They will describe a typical day on the plantation, which puts things in perspective as far as what we have now. From a mobility standpoint, it was very tough to walk through the plantation. In the 1600s, there weren't any laws mandating accessibility for persons with disabilities, so we had to put up with the situation for what it was, because the entire 17th–century experience had to be reenacted.

Everyone was extremely fascinated by the Pilgrim actors, who made us feel right at home. I suppose that each person in our group wanted to focus on different aspects of the plantation. Usually when something like this happens in a large group on a field trip, the group tends to split up. In this case, our group was large, with about 14 of us, and the students with little or no vision were normally accompanied by the teacher or students with more vision.

It was foggy, damp, and drizzly on the afternoon of our trip to the Plymouth Plantation, and for a large portion of the tour, I was accompanied by Jennie, who had a lot more vision than I had. At one point, as I was walking with Jennie on the plantation grounds, we noticed that the rest of the group was gone! Neither one of us was nervous about our situation. We had faith that the rest of the group was not far away. However, minutes went by, and there was still no sign of the others.

It is very tough to describe what was going through my mind at that moment, but I'll give it a try. Here I was, with the most popular girl at Perkins, all alone on the Plymouth Plantation, while I was cautiously optimistic that we would be found eventually. You must also realize that I was 18. How many boys that age, in this particular situation, wouldn't wonder if it would be hours before they were found? Don't worry; I had more faith in our rescue than that, but I think you get my point. As Jennie and I were walking around the grounds by ourselves, she began to express our predicament verbally. I did not need to try to be calm. For whatever reason, I *was* calm, so no effort needed to be made.

All at once, one of the other girls found Jennie and me, and motioned to several others that everything was all right. Soon the group was back together again, and the experience of getting lost with the most popular girl on campus was an eventful memory.

In 1976, Perkins took advantage of every opportunity to celebrate the Bicentennial with the rest of the country. The drama club and chorus combined to do a 200–year history of America, featuring songs, reenactments of historical events, and comments from characters who had lived through these events. Our history teacher played a major role in these celebrations by taking us on a trip along the Freedom Trail. This trail featured lots of memorabilia from the Revolutionary War and was scattered throughout Greater Boston, where tourists relived the actual happenings of that time in our history. We needed to go on two separate days, but even though we skipped two days of school in order to tour the Freedom Trail, I still don't think we saw it all. We spent a lot of time on the MBTA traveling between stops. Sometimes we had to stand up while the train or trolley was moving. We had no choice, as the vehicle was overcrowded.

During our first day on the Freedom Trail, we stopped for lunch and had to eat outdoors. Though it was the middle of January, that didn't prevent a large flock of birds from flying all around me while I was casually eating my sandwich. I felt like I was in an Alfred Hitchcock movie.

One of my favorite parts of the Freedom Trail was when we put our personal information into a computer in order to determine whether we were Loyalists or members of any other party affiliation from the 18th century. We also went to Charlestown, Revere, and other areas around Boston, where events from 200 years before were reenacted. Our teacher spent so much time with us on the Freedom Trail that the Santa Letter Committee gave him a tour guide's job as a joke for Christmas.

In May of 1976, our history teacher took us on two field trips in one week. On Monday, May 3, we went to Mystic Seaport in Connecticut, and on Thursday, May 6, we visited Old Sturbridge Village. On the way back from Mystic Seaport, as I was holding an ice cream cone in my hand, the driver hit a bump in the road, causing the ice cream to spill into my sock. Old Sturbridge Village is similar to Plymouth Plantation structurally and environmentally, but there aren't any actors who tell their stories as if they were living in the past.

I'm not certain if Perkins offers this today, but back in the 1970s, the Yacht Club arranged boat trips up and down the Charles River once a year for those students who were interested. The Charles River flows west of Boston and right by the southern end of the Perkins campus. Along with the boat ride, organizers put on a picnic, giving everyone a chance to socialize and have fun before leaving school for the summer.

Chapter 20

Life in the Cottage

Most children who go to school in their home towns live with their families. I will assume that the average number of children in a household is approximately two or three, so that if someone has seven or eight brothers and sisters, it's considered a very large family. Children with large families may find their living spaces a bit crowded, but that doesn't compare to life in the cottages at Perkins.

Naturally, the Perkins cottages are much bigger than even a large family's house, but the number of kids that one lives with at Perkins is much larger. For those children who live on campus, especially those who stay on weekends, they are like a second family to one another. There are fights, good times, practical jokes, games, disciplining by the superiors, and anything else that would take place in a normal home with parents and children.

In my case, as an only child, I went from being the only boy in the house to one of 37 boys in a cottage. With these 37 boys, there were 37 different personalities, 37 different issues, 37 attitudes, and 37 levels of respect. With that said, I got along with most of the boys, although several of them used to get under my skin at times. In Potter, we were all between the ages of 10 and 15. In other words, kids are kids, and you have to expect them to behave as such.

I've already described a typical day in the Lower School, including the basics of what we did in Potter Cottage. But now I'd like to dive deeper into the lifestyles and relationships we all had.

During my two years in Potter, I probably had nearly 20 roommates, because the housemothers switched my bedroom eight times. Though I never understood the reason for all these moves, it gave me an opportunity to get to know a variety of roommates and their personal habits. I've already talked about Vic, the *Star Trek* fanatic, and George, the *Sesame Street* fanatic. I had two roommates who were deaf and blind, so it was very hard to communicate with either one of them, since I didn't know sign language. Sometimes, if I raised my voice while the deaf child faced me, he would probably understand part of what I said, but there was never any guarantee.

One of the deaf boys used to call me Mick. For the life of me, I don't know how he concluded that my name was Mick, but he did. Eventually, he was told what my real name was, and he even said it correctly, Bobby Branco. But right after that, he went back to calling me Mick.

While many of my roommates were like me, talking a little at bedtime and then going to sleep, because they knew they had to get up early in the morning, other roommates were absolute riots. One boy spent a lot of time breaking wind in order to get a rise out of his roommates.

In the Upper School, where some of the boys believed that they had more freedom after bed check, they visited other boys' rooms so that they could talk and listen to the radio. Bed check was at 10:00, but obviously, it didn't mean much to some kids. Sure, they were in bed at 10:00, but out of bed at 10:05, ready to go bedroom–hopping. I tried not to get involved with that. Aside from believing I'd get caught by a cottage staff member if I visited my friends after bed check, I regarded myself as someone who needed a good night's sleep, because I knew that I had a full day ahead: up at 6:30, breakfast at 7:00, bed made, clothes on, homework done, school all day, activities at night, etc.

Despite my own philosophy about sleep, I was not spared from the all night chatter. There were many nights when my roommate, Mickey, would invite his friends into the bedroom after hours, or his friends would come in voluntarily. I tried telling these boys that I needed my sleep, but though I acted very mature when I made my request, and I had a valid reason for asking them to keep quiet, the boys ignored my request and kept talking. Sometimes the conversations would go on past midnight.

These night owls would listen to music, and occasionally they would tune into *Mystery Theater*. I was not very happy about this. I thought about reporting these incidents to the cottage staff, or at least throwing the visitors out of the bedroom. After all, the room was just as much mine as it was Mickey's. However, it was obvious that I was being disrespected, because it was all about what the others wanted to do, so anything else I would say or do wouldn't help my reputation.

Though I tried to socialize when I felt it was appropriate, I was often thought of as a geek who only wanted to think about his studies. That label was a bit unfair. I was trying to be a normal boy in an abnormal situation. Socializing was great, but school was more important. If I hadn't paid attention to what the teachers wanted me to do, and if I hadn't taken care of myself properly, I might not have passed some of my courses. As far as yapping far into the night is concerned, perhaps those boys felt they could function all day on less than six hours of sleep, but I didn't want to be one of them. The clincher was when a British boy from New Jersey came to Perkins for an evaluation and just happened to sleep in my bedroom. To my surprise, and even to Mickey's, this guy talked until three in the morning.

While most of the food at Perkins was nutritious and traditional, there were some foods that were out of the ordinary. For breakfast, we had a variety of cereals, including the two hot ones, cream of wheat and oatmeal. Our second course usually consisted of eggs of all types, toast, bacon, and pancakes or French toast. Sometimes we had different types of muffins, such as English, corn, blueberry, and bran. Coffee cake and Danish pastries were also on the menu from time to time. We had our glass of milk and a smaller glass of a different fruit juice each morning. At our place setting, we were each given a vitamin pill, which was placed inside the bowl of our spoon.

We had our meat, potato, and vegetables most days of the week for lunch, with one day a week designated for fish. Normally, Thursdays were fish days, but during Lent, we had fish on Fridays.

Suppers were pretty ordinary, but occasionally we had delectable delights which perhaps you would not eat in your own homes.

Let's start out by talking about delicious creamed chipped beef on toast. Though some of the boys thought it was horrible, I'm not one of them. I was very glad to have the opportunity to be introduced to it, and found it to be quite satisfying to the palate. My mouth waters just thinking about how tender the chipped beef was, with creamy gravy all over it.

Another Perkins special was rarebit, also known as Welsh rabbit. The best way to describe Welsh rabbit is to tell you that it's melted cheese, sometimes seasoned, then poured over crackers or toast. I've often wondered why they called this concoction rabbit, Welsh or otherwise. I don't remember the cheese having two long ears protruding from the top while lying flat on the piece of toast in our plates. I challenge anyone to convince me that it filled us up, because believe me, it didn't.

Then there was the number one love/hate meal, liver and onions. I don't know anyone who casually liked or disliked it; they either adored it madly or despised it terribly. I loved it, and still do, no matter who makes it.

Hash was another popular item at Perkins. Though we usually ate it once a week, it took years before we heard an interesting rumor about *why* we were served it. Apparently, the cooks took all of the uneaten leftovers from previous meals, then turned it into hash for Thursday night suppers.

For dessert, we were offered a number of classy delights, such as gingerbread, apple brown betty, trifle, apple crisp, an assortment of puddings, cherry cobbler, and other favorites.

In the Perkins cottages, we had our share of entertainment. Several of the Lower School boys decided to form a small band one day so that they could put on a concert in Potter. They used their musical talents and wild imaginations in order to concoct their own versions of classic songs. Most of us listened in awe while my friend Alex and his partners changed the title and words of a famous song by Santana. They called it "You Got to Change Your Evil Ways, Perkins." One boy played the piano, while another had a makeshift drum. After we had enjoyed several creative tunes and lyrics, the concert was abruptly halted by Mrs. Anderson, who probably felt that enough was enough. I really don't know what happened for sure, or what was actually said to these musicians, but there are times when a semblance of order must return to an environment with 37 boys in it.

In Upper School, we had our guitarists and pianists as well. Only this time, it wasn't staff members who put a stop to the piano playing; it was another bunch of boys who wanted to watch television. In Bridgman, Tompkins, and Moulton, the piano was situated 20 feet from the TV set, so that when we wanted to play a tune, it bothered television watchers. For a period of time in Tompkins, usually before lunch and supper, my friends Pedro and Cal would spend several minutes playing songs by Charlie Rich, Credence Clearwater Revival, and other classic pop music stars.

It was fun to listen to if you weren't concentrating on something else, but one day, Pedro and Cal met their match. Juan and a teacher trainee were trying to watch television, and they finally decided to confront the pianists once and for all. There was a war of words among the foursome about who had been in the sitting room first: those who wanted to play the piano or those who wanted to watch TV. In my opinion, the problem would have been solved if there had been a partition built between the piano and the TV set in order to block out sound.

At times, I tried to play songs from the Top 40 on the piano. I recall three songs that I tried to play back then: "Tubular Bells," which is the theme from *The Exorcist*; "I Can Help," by Billy Swan; and "Gee Baby," which was performed by Peter Shelley. Sometimes boys would practice the song "Dueling Banjos," using the lower and higher sections of the piano keyboard to replace the banjo and guitar. Pedro and I also used to make up our own renditions of songs from TV commercials.

One day in my Senior year, when Pedro asked me to accompany him to the Northeast Building so he could see his girlfriend and her friends, we heard a very imaginative percussion duet between Pedro's girlfriend and her friend Rita. Rita was playing a pot, while Pedro's girl played the spoons.

So, to put this all in general terms, Perkins students tried very hard to demonstrate musical talent, whether they actually had it or merely wanted to have it. In all seriousness, there was a boy who played the drums as well as the professionals. After school, Bill would place his drums backstage in Dwight Hall, and when he knew everyone had left the vicinity, he practiced. He was fabulous on the drums, and people heard his performance throughout the entire Howe building and beyond. However, I pitied anyone who tried to do their homework in the study halls during Bill's drum practices, because they were in the direct line of fire.

For those students and staff who smoked, Upper School cottages had a smoking room. Yes, even blind people smoke, and they don't need any help doing it. Since I have always been a nonsmoker, this was one room I never graced with my presence.

A man named Stephen Blaisdell attended Perkins approximately a century ago. He didn't have much money, but he vowed that he would be a success one day. When his dream came true, Blaisdell became extremely wealthy, so much so that he decided to give Perkins an endowment. The idea was for the children at Perkins to receive a small portion of this fund for years to come and to spend it any way they pleased. The fund was distributed very carefully and creatively. Twice a year, each student was given a Blaisdell dollar as a gift. We would find them at our place settings in the dining room, and we always felt very proud to have an extra dollar in our pocket to spend. I'm not sure whether Mr. Blaisdell's endowment has run out yet, but whether it has or not, he made thousands of children very happy.

Life in the cottage wasn't always peaches and cream, and I don't mean a popular dessert. Sometimes we thought of punishment as abuse, while other times, boys were dealt with on a rational, logical level. Regarding punishment, it usually depended on who was doing the punishing rather than what the offense was. For example, during my Senior year, several of the younger seventh–graders were accused of breaking some pool equipment in Moulton Cottage. Mr. Acres, who was housemaster at the time, didn't know who did it, but he knew that the seventh–grade boys liked to play pool. When he found out about the broken equipment, he summoned the younger boys to the pool table and demanded to know what had happened and who had done it. Apparently the boys did not satisfy Mr. Acres by confessing or squealing on one of their friends. So, under those circumstances, you couldn't really blame Mr. Acres for his subsequent action. I believe he asked the group not to go near the pool table for a week or so.

While Mr. Acres' disciplinary action against these seventh-graders was appropriate, given the lack of cooperation by the young group, I'm now going to talk about a more ridiculous action which affected an entire cottage. It took place in Tompkins Cottage while I was a high school Sophomore. Most of the boys were in their rooms, downstairs, or out of the cottage, doing what they normally did. It appeared to be a very ordinary day, with no unforeseen catastrophes on the horizon. I remember being in my bedroom listening to the radio when all at once, someone opened the door, asking me to report to the bathroom.

Before I had a chance to ask myself why I had to report to the upstairs bathroom, especially since I hadn't been there in several hours, I learned that every boy in Tompkins had been summoned. Obviously, something major had taken place, and someone was very anxious to get to the bottom of it, so the only way he knew how to figure it out was to find as many of the boys as possible and bring them inside the bathroom.

So, there we all were, congregating in the large, smelly upstairs bathroom, while the assistant housemaster, Mr. Riley, gave us all a lecture. Apparently, someone had put too much paper in the toilet bowl, causing the waste to back up. From my perspective, I knew I had more important and exciting things to do that day than stand in a smelly bathroom like a five-year-old being scolded by his father. No matter how much we were overcome by that awful smell of human waste material, we all had to stand there while Mr. Riley reminded us that when we were through taking a shit, we shouldn't overuse the toilet paper. Those were his words, not mine. By the way, Mr. Riley is a minister.

Though I hope the guilty party got the message, I wonder if Mr. Riley couldn't have handled the issue in a different way. It's true that no one knew who had blocked the toilet, but rather than bring us all into the stinky bathroom to lecture us, I feel he should have made an announcement in the dining room about the proper treatment of the toilet. I'm sure, as teenagers, we would have appreciated and respected Mr. Riley's concerns and recommendations without him shoving it in our faces. Even though the bathroom incident was, in my opinion, very stupid, I understand what Mr. Riley was trying to do. He hoped that the guilty boy would be embarrassed enough not to block the toilet ever again.

On another occasion, a deaf–blind boy in Tompkins got mad and pulled a button off his shirt. Mrs. Anderson, the housemother, was just as mad, and she proceeded to rip the rest of the shirt. I don't know if the boy apologized, or if he reacted at all, but I know I would have had no problem asking Mrs. Anderson to buy me a new shirt, no matter what kind of trouble I was in, and if I hadn't asked her to buy the shirt, I'd have had my parents ask her. To my mind, this particular punishment bordered on abusive treatment. There was no question in my mind about that. It's one thing to spend 10 minutes in a stinky bathroom while you hear a staff member talk about something you know you didn't do, but it's quite another thing when a housemother ruins your shirt because she didn't like how you pulled a button off it. All someone had to do was sew it back on. I think Mrs. Anderson had hung around Miss Jones too long.

At Perkins, some of the boys picked up on others' quirks, including those of staff members, even to the point where the boys would copy these particular quirks. As I mentioned earlier, most of the Perkins staff either lived in a cottage or ate in one for lunch. For several months, the director of personnel ate lunch with us. He was a very classy, formal, no–nonsense man who expected everyone to conform to his standards. I'm not implying that his standards were wrong. In fact, I admired his thoughtfulness, and wish that there were more people like him today who cared about how the kids dress for school, how they should keep themselves clean, how they cut their meat, etc.

When the Perkins personnel director saw someone having a tough time cutting his meat at the lunch table, he would say to the boy in a slight German accent, "Cut it!" Every once in a while, someone at the table had a problem cutting his meat, so the personnel director used that expression again and again. It got to the point where several of the boys began to impersonate the man, walking around the campus saying, "Cut it, cut it!" One day, my friend Mickey, the boy who invited his friends into the bedroom at all hours of the night, decided to be a daredevil. As he was walking by the personnel director's office on the way to class one day, he yelled out, "Cut it!"

Cottage life also gave boys the opportunity to confide in one another about their hopes, dreams, and desires. A few boys wished they could leave Perkins, while others wanted to beat up their worst enemy or take him in a wrestling match. However, life in the cottage would not be complete without the boys talking about their favorite girls. Not that I kept score, or anything like that, but it seemed that Jennie, my classmate, was indeed the most talked-about girl in the cottage. If my memory serves me correctly, at least seven or eight boys were interested in her at one time or another.

My friend Pedro, though he was one of my best friends, was not a very good confider. For example, when his feelings were hurt, he kept things bottled up, because he didn't want to talk about what was bothering him. With all the sharing of hopes and dreams came their abrupt end at the sound of the early bell, which meant another day of heavy-duty school and extracurricular activity.

Sometimes when the boys talked about their desires, they

infused gossip about other students and their private affairs, which made me wonder if these boys were jealous and wished they could do the same things that the students they were gossiping about allegedly did. For example, I heard a rather bizarre story about a boy and a girl in the rec room. Supposedly, the girl was sitting on the boy's lap for nearly a half hour, trying to arouse him sexually. When it seemed as though the boy was satisfied, the girl allegedly said, "A little more, please."

Now what was I supposed to think of a story like that? In those days, students were suspended for kissing, so if a couple had done what was described to me in a public place like the rec room, they must have either led an extremely charmed life or had a lot of political connections. Or the boy had made the whole thing up. For decades I believed that the story was false, until I heard it again last year from a different source while at a Perkins reunion. Now I wonder.

If you think that story was incredible, I can top it by far. One evening, as I was lying in bed, my roommate Larry came in like a tornado, proud to tell me something that he had allegedly seen. Before I describe what he supposedly witnessed, I must tell you that if he expected me to believe it, he was running the risk of having several of his friends in deep trouble with the authorities.

Behind Brooks Cottage was a large hill where the kids would go sledding. Well, on the night in question, Larry claimed he was near Brooks Hill, watching six couples in action, and the exercises they were performing had nothing to do with tobogganing. Without hesitation, Larry told me that each one of the six couples was having sex. He described the positions they were in, the location of each sexual act, and the names of each couple doing it.

So picture this in your own mind. I was supposed to believe that brave Larry stood on Brooks Hill while he watched 12 of his friends having sex. He knew the rules at Perkins, yet he trusted me enough to risk the futures of all these boys and girls. How did he know that I wasn't going to rat them out to the principal, the director, or one of the deans? Then again, he probably thought that I wasn't too stupid to realize that he had made the whole thing up, and he figured I'd laugh it off, as he might have done. The part of his story that made me question its validity was that he had supposedly been there, but without a companion of his own. Why would a boy watch six couples have sex and then report it to me? I asked him that question, but being the drama king he sometimes was, he insisted that the story was true. I doubt it was true, but if it was, then I would have to say that despite Perkins' attempts at protecting its student body, orgies weren't out of the realm of possibility.

Chapter 21

Independent Living

Prior to my Junior year in high school, the only time I spent in the Northeast Building was for Sunday night suppers. Many of the cottage staff members were off duty on weekends, which meant that most of the boys and girls ate on neutral territory where everything was prepared and served under one roof, cafeteria–style. In the early 1970s, the Northeast Building became the place where the older boys would learn how to take care of their own apartments. Though I commend Perkins for giving us this opportunity, you must also bear in mind that we still had our academic responsibilities, especially those of us who were preparing for college.

The Northeast Building was larger than the other cottages in the area, but not too many of the students had their bedrooms on the same floors there. The reason for this was that the Northeast Building had four floors.

On September 7, 1975, my experience in the Northeast Building began. While I describe the cottage and what we were asked to do, it's going to sound as though this was our life. In a sense, it would have been if we had been running our own households, but in our case, as I said earlier, we were also students. The majority of the boys who lived in the Northeast Building at the time were Juniors, Seniors, or young adults who had returned to Perkins so that they could learn more about independent living.

As I began the process of unpacking for the first time in the Northeast Building, two things which had never happened before became evident. First, I learned I would be sharing a suite with three other boys, and second, I was given a key to the main door of the suite. My suite was on the fourth floor, across the hall from another. So there were eight boys living in two suites.

As you walked into a suite, you would be in the main sitting room. Adjacent to the sitting room were two bedrooms and a bathroom. Each bedroom had two beds with no legs. The mattress was placed on a wooden slab with a drawer on each side, and included in the bedding was the dreaded fitted sheet. Those of you who have to make your beds with fitted sheets have my deepest sympathy. I prefer the regular flat sheets, with which you can make hospital corners, which Miss Tully taught us how to do way back in Lower School.

Another form of culture shock was that there would be no bell waking us up at 6:30, the way it did while we were in the other cottages. As a result, the boys had to bring their own alarm clocks to the Northeast Building, or they would probably oversleep.

It wasn't long before I found out who my roommate was going to be. Alas! It was Mickey, the boy who had invited his friends into the bedroom we had shared in Tompkins. I hoped deep down that now that Mickey was a bit older, he would have the sense not to invite the other members of our suite into the bedroom after hours. Well, as Aerosmith said, Dream On! But I'll get to all that later.

Mickey and I shared one of the bedrooms in our suite, while Brent and Wallace shared the other. Across the hall, four other boys shared the second suite. Most of us were high school Juniors and Seniors, about to embark on one of the busiest times in our lives.

So there we all were, each with our own key to a suite on the fourth floor of the Northeast Building. It wasn't long before we were given our assigned chores. Each one of the four boys in their suite had two major jobs, a job in the suite and a job in the bedroom. Every other week, for example, it was my turn to vacuum my bedroom, which was carpeted. During the alternate week, it was Mickey's turn. In the other bedroom, Brent vacuumed one week, and Wallace the next. At the same time, each one of the four of us, Brent, Wallace, Mickey, and I, had to clean the bathroom once a month. That way, since there were four of us, the bathroom was cleaned each week. By the way, our housemother happened to be Mrs. Anderson, whom most of us knew from Potter and Tompkins. Given that we were much older, she treated us like older teenagers, though we still had to follow the cottage rules.

The suites on the third floor of the Northeast Building were occupied by young adults who had either returned to Perkins after graduation or who had come there for the first time to brush up on their independent living skills. I hardly knew these guys, because many were new. The second floor consisted of the housemaster's apartment, and probably Mrs. Anderson's, though I never had to find that out.

As you walked into the Northeast Building, you would see a ping pong table on your left and the sitting room on your right. Several boys played ping pong, and they played it well. Sometimes we joked with the boys when a ping pong ball got loose and rolled on the large floor in the front entrance. The sitting room was furnished with a piano, a television set, and a long couch with a coffee table. As you walked straight ahead from the entrance, you entered the dining room. Beyond the dining room was an area where snacks were put out each night in case the boys were hungry after a long, hard day. Despite the fact that we lived in the Northeast Building so that we would learn how to keep up our own apartments, we didn't make our own meals; they were served three times a day in the dining room.

While we all adjusted to our new lives, especially in our suites, some of us made a scientific project out of vacuuming. When the vacuum cleaner was completely set up, one end was connected to a large vent in one of the bedroom walls. If you put your face up to the vent and talked loud enough, people downstairs could respond to you through another vent, making this a communications system of sorts.

As I pointed out in an earlier chapter, Mickey wasn't the type to go to sleep right away at night. In Tompkins, he invited his friends into the bedroom, which kept me from doing what was best for me, sleeping. In the Northeast Building, Mickey listened to the radio for a while after bedtime, so one day we both agreed that he should wear a set of headphones so that I wouldn't be kept awake. I only shared the room with Mickey until February of 1976, when he left Perkins for public school. The unofficial story about Mickey's departure was that he had enough sight to drive a car. In the suite, Mickey was replaced by Larry, the boy who told me about the sex on the hill.

As long as we all knew our responsibilities in the Northeast Building, while also fulfilling our obligations to our teachers and organization directors, our school year ran smoothly. I guess you could say that the living situation in the Northeast Building resembled assisted living, because while we took care of our own suites, we were offered three meals each day, as we were previously in the other cottages.

With that said, something happened during our stay in the Northeast Building which prompted the staff to give us another job. I don't want you to get the wrong impression. The job we were asked to do didn't offer any pay, but the staff, for some reason, felt it was necessary. That is, each boy was assigned to phone duty. His job was to stay in the cottage during the assigned period of time, and when the phone rang, he would answer it and summon the person whom the phone call was for. From what I remember, phone duty was met with a negative reaction, because it meant that we'd have even less time for our own social activities, and more time to sit around waiting for the phone to ring.

Well, as luck would have it, I was assigned Sunday evenings from 6:00 to 10:00. For me, Sunday nights were social nights, because I made sure I had no homework to do then, and there weren't any extracurricular activities going on except when we had to rehearse for a concert. Nevertheless, as soon as supper was over on Sundays, I needed to stay inside.

I remember the first Sunday night on phone duty. I had my little transistor radio with me in the sitting room so that I could occupy the time listening to my favorite sports talk show, *Calling All Sports*, with Ken Beatrice. It was 6:00, but I enjoyed the sports show enough to sustain my patience while I waited for the phone to ring. Soon it was 6:30, and the phone hadn't rung yet. Then it was 7:00, 8:00, 9:00. No phone calls. By now, I had had enough. I had been sitting on the couch for three hours waiting for a phone call, and I suddenly had a strong urge to do the things I wanted to do. To make the situation even more tempting, there weren't any staff members around. I left the sitting room and proceeded to go upstairs with my radio. I unlocked the door to my suite and went into the bedroom.

Moments after I had settled in, there was a knock at my door. Well, wouldn't you know it; the assistant housemaster, Chipper, had come to get me. When I opened the bedroom door, Chipper said to me in a very calm but stern voice, "Get your ass downstairs." By now, my shift was almost over anyway, and I had already endured three hours of boredom, so I had no problem finishing my shift.

The danger in assigning different boys to different phone duty shifts was that there was a lot of switching off. If a boy didn't like his shift, he would secretly go to another boy and ask to change shifts with him. The only time the boys were caught doing that was when a member of the staff saw a different boy on duty than the one marked in the book. In all honesty, phone duty did not last very long, either because the staff felt that it wasn't necessary anymore, or because the boys simply didn't feel like being confined to the cottage all night to wait for a phone call. We had lots of other responsibilities: four or five subjects of homework, working with readers, writing essays, rehearsing for plays and concerts, taking care of our suites, playing sports, etc., so wasting time in front of a phone didn't help our cause. It's possible that the cottage staff knew this, too, and if that was true, I commend them.

Aside from the phone not ringing very often during our shifts, another frustrating part of phone duty was not knowing where everyone was. There were at least five staff members and 16 boys living in the cottage, but it wasn't as if they all told me where they would be in case the phone calls were for them. It wasn't as though we were actual receptionists, and on the flip side, I don't think most of the boys wanted to report to their peers about where they were going to be all evening. They didn't have to report to a staff member as long as they were back in the cottage by 10:00, so why would they feel obligated to tell their friends where they were going, if they even knew that ahead of time?

In June, my time in the Northeast Building came to an end, and as it turned out, so did my busiest year at Perkins. When we returned the following September, which was the start of my Senior and final year, I was placed in Moulton, a traditional boys' cottage. After all the responsibilities in the Northeast Building, I regarded Moulton Cottage as dessert; no more vacuuming, no more bathroom maintenance, and no more boxed beds with fitted sheets. It was a normal year in the cottage, though I knew deep down that this was going to be my last year at Perkins. The Seniors were reminded of that fact all the time, because part of what they had to do was to prepare for graduation, as well as for life after Perkins. In my case, my guidance counselor and other interested parties, including the Massachusetts Commission for the Blind, helped me plan for the future based on my goal, which was to attend college.

In April of 1977, I was surprised to learn that my life in Moulton Cottage was going to be interrupted for five weeks. The director of Keller–Sullivan Cottage, the place where many of us lived independently for a time, informed me that it was my turn to live there. Keller–Sullivan was similar to the Northeast Building, but in Keller–Sullivan, you had to cook your own meals and do your own shopping, as well as take care of your rooms. Again, we were supposed to be focused on independent living, as we were in the Northeast Building, but despite all of that, we had our other responsibilities as well.

That April, two months before I graduated, I had to fill out mission statements and college applications, rehearse for the spring concert, do homework in five major subjects, go food shopping, cook two meals a day, and do weekly laundry. How many of you, in all honesty, can handle that load for five weeks and say with confidence that you did every one of those things well? I can't promise you that I did. All I know is that on Sunday, April 24, 1977, I prepared for my five-week stay in Keller–Sullivan.

When the students went to Keller–Sullivan for their independent living, they spent Sunday nights in their original cottages, and the other four nights in Keller–Sullivan. So for five weeks, my Sunday nights were spent in Moulton. You can imagine all the packing and unpacking I had to do, making sure I had clothes at Keller–Sullivan, Moulton, and home.

The staff at Keller–Sullivan, for the most part, knew our

difficulties and did their best to make our lives run smoothly. For example, on the first day, my cooking teacher took me shopping after school and assisted me with my list. This was another first, because up to that point, we had simply eaten what was served. Now, for the first time, I made my own food-buying decisions. Quite often during my five–week stay in Keller–Sullivan, because of all my other obligations, I didn't cook anything that took a long time. I remember making TV dinners for supper on numerous occasions, and instant breakfast at least two mornings per week. I had my lunch in Moulton, thanking God for a break.

My time in Keller–Sullivan offered another first for me; it was the first time at Perkins that I lived with girls. There were approximately three girls and two boys in the independent living program at that time, but we were all supervised by teachers. The girls lived downstairs and the boys lived upstairs. Though this was my first time in a mixed cottage, there really wasn't time to do much socializing. We were all like ships that passed in the night, coming in from chorus rehearsals or scholastic obligations and then leaving early in the morning to report to study hall or chapel.

It was then that I realized the value of instant breakfast and TV dinners, other than their nutritional value. We had to live a fast–paced life, and there was absolutely nothing we could do about it.

However, one evening, a young supervisor thought she could do something about it, at least where I was concerned. It was the end of supper, and I had to get to an important chorus rehearsal for the spring concert that year. The chorus teacher was strict, as most teachers would be in these situations. You needed to be at the rehearsal by 7:00.

It was already bad enough that I couldn't spend the evening doing my homework; I had to shuttle between supper cleanup and a chorus rehearsal, with homework being third on the priority list. To sum it up, I was already frustrated because I had to get to rehearsal, when I would rather have gone to study hall to do homework after supper cleanup, because at least I wouldn't be under pressure to get to study hall at a certain time. I would get there when I could, and then I would use my remaining time to concentrate on homework.

Not that night, however. I had to be with the chorus at 7:00. The young female supervisor, Miss Carroll, saw that I had other things on my mind while I was cleaning off the kitchen table after supper. I knew it was getting close to the time when I had to leave to get to the rehearsal, and I pointed that out. Well, Miss Carroll wouldn't let me leave.

You can count all the things I was mad about at one time. First, I couldn't do my homework because of chorus rehearsal, and now I couldn't leave for chorus rehearsal, because Miss Carroll insisted that I finish cleaning up. If I satisfied Miss Carroll, the chorus teacher would be mad because of my late arrival, and if I didn't have time to do the homework I wanted to do because of chorus, then my teachers would be mad. So, I had to decide who should be the most angry: me, Miss Carroll, my academic teachers, or the chorus teacher.

Well, the decision was easy. I knew it wasn't going to be me, because anger combined with lots of responsibility causes stress. I also knew that it wasn't going to be my academic teachers or the chorus teacher, because I didn't feel like being reprimanded publicly. So I decided that if anyone was going to be mad that night, it would be Miss Carroll. She was young, and occasionally she acted like a peer instead of a superior. For example, I must have told her at least five times that I had to go, and each time, she'd say things like, "Oh, no you don't!" -- things that 12–year–olds would say. When I realized that Miss Carroll was apparently something of a tease, I got the best of her and managed to leave Keller–Sullivan in time for the chorus rehearsal. Later, I must have found time to do whatever homework I was given.

So, here's the picture. While I was preparing for graduation, I had to worry about school, chorus, homework, cooking, shopping, cleaning, and all the unexpected things that came up in between. When the five weeks of independent living were over, I felt like the astronauts during a splashdown. I thought to myself, *Thank God it's over!*

Chapter 22

Anticipation and Conclusions

To this day, there have been numerous discussions about how Perkins prepared us for the outside world. Some believe that where we spent years living with, studying with, eating with, and socializing with only the blind, we weren't properly prepared to face a sighted world.

In my opinion, there are two sides to this very interesting debate. On the one hand, Perkins did its best to teach us how to be switchboard operators, transcribers, receptionists, salespeople, and babysitters. They also gave us an opportunity to tune pianos, play musical instruments, sing, act, shop, cook, clean, and do laundry. All of these tasks are performed in the outside world by sighted as well as blind individuals.

I guess those who take the opposite viewpoint would talk about the intangibles. While it's true that we were taught a lot of skills, we weren't taught how to face certain uphill battles. We weren't taught how to advocate for and sell ourselves. We weren't prepared for the constant discrimination and rejection we'd have to face outside of school while competing with the sighted for jobs.

If we're going to accuse Perkins of not fully preparing us for life with the sighted despite all the skills we were taught, I don't think you can put that kind of label on Perkins if the staff didn't actually have the knowledge or the means to prepare us for the college of hard knocks. The staff, in my opinion, tried its best to guide us through the necessary process to prepare us for college or a career. My readers read the college catalogs for me, because the catalogs were not brailled. The guidance counselors, for the most part, did what they could. However, in all fairness, the teachers and guidance counselors, especially the sighted ones, did not have the experiences we were about to have after we graduated, because you'd really have to be blind in order to appreciate all of life's uphill battles that I just talked about.

Looking back, I suppose I could have had more conversations with the blind teachers in order to find out about their own experiences after they had left school. Many of those teachers had been educated at Perkins. One of my math teachers, my Spanish teacher, an elementary school teacher, and a special needs teacher are all blind, and they graduated from Perkins before they became teachers there, so I'm sure they knew all about the culture shock that comes with going from a blind environment to a sighted one.

You might say, "They're blind teachers in a school with blind students. What would they know about a sighted environment?" Well, my guess is that when they weren't working, they traveled with the sighted, shopped with the sighted, went to church with the sighted, and dated or married the sighted.

My friend Ralph, the extremely self–sufficient blind father I referred to earlier who was taken out of swimming class because of an abusive instructor, tells me to this day that I show the effects of being at Perkins, because I appear sheltered. If Perkins caused me to develop a sheltered personality, that's not my fault. But then again, how could Perkins make you act sheltered for the rest of your life, especially if you went there during a time when the institutional environment was changing drastically? In my opinion, people, blind or sighted, act sheltered either because they want to be sheltered or because they are pampered and overprotected by family members, and not because they spent years at a private school for the blind.

Perkins offered strict campus rules, rules that many of us complained about. But when those rules were slightly relaxed during my eight–year stay, many students were allowed to show their true independent selves, bad or good. I don't think that those who smuggled booze onto the campus, robbed from the campus, had sex in the bowling alley, traveled to Watertown Square, cleaned their cottage suites, made their own meals, or took care of the staff's children were exactly sheltered.

I host three reunions a year of former Perkins students, and based on my conversations with dozens of my friends, I would say that most do not act sheltered. Many are living on their own, are married or live with partners, have children, and do lots of traveling. Those who are sheltered were more than likely coddled by family members as children. How often have I said that Perkins housemothers had to deprogram certain behaviors, because they didn't like how some of the kids acted or how some of them didn't know how to do simple tasks, such as cutting their meat or tying their shoes?

Perkins did not shelter Everett. His mother coddled and pitied him after he tragically lost his sight at age nine. Perkins did not shelter the blind boy who had his shoes tied for him at home by his little sister at their mother's direction. His mother did that. Shelterism is a trait based on your individual background. The Perkins student who was so afraid of becoming pregnant after a boy kissed her on the lips was obviously naive about the subject, but was that Perkins' fault? For every teenaged Perkins girl who didn't know how babies were conceived, other Perkins girls were getting pregnant, and they knew exactly what they were doing.

Those who wish to judge Perkins are free to call it whatever they want. But can you imagine what would have happened if Perkins hadn't been a so-called shelter, given all the thefts, drugs, drinking, and sex that went on anyway among the students who were supposedly sheltered? Ralph would say that I was sheltered because I didn't learn about most of life's hard knocks or how to be street smart. He feels I don't always handle people the right way, and therefore it relates to shelterism. Ralph did drugs, had sex with hundreds of women, spent a night in jail, and was a bar-hopper. He can say I'm sheltered all he wants, but I would much rather be who I am than who he was, even though he's turned his life around. I think the perception is that Perkins sheltered us because we were all blind students living in a blind community, making our environment a shelter.

In addition to all that I just said, there were also several members of the Perkins staff who felt they should play God with our futures, because they didn't trust our judgment of what we wanted to do after we left school. As early as the middle of my Junior year, I knew that I wanted to go to college and learn more about computers. At the time, I was very fascinated by the Perkins computer. It's now a dinosaur, but nonetheless, it was a computer that you could program to do many things, and I enjoyed that. I remember applying to my local college and filling out a mission statement for the Massachusetts Commission for the Blind, because if they were going to help me through college financially, I had to come up with a convincing goal for them to work with in order to make the ultimate decision as to whether they would fund my college courses.

Because I had such a focus on the field of computers, I made the mistake of applying to the College of Engineering at the local university, because it sounded like the appropriate field. In 1977, what did I know? When I went to the admissions office at my local university to tell them I wanted to apply to the College of Engineering in order to study the computer, the admissions representative practically laughed in my face. But at the same time, he kindly straightened me out about my misguided goal. Engineering is engineering, and not necessarily computer programming. If I wanted to take computer courses, I had to apply to the College of Business.

By the way, the admissions director, even though I did not pursue engineering, made it a point to tell me how extremely difficult it would be for me to become a blind engineer. I guess you could call that my first taste of life outside of Perkins, even though I still had a few more months before I graduated.

While I was exploring college life, my Perkins guidance counselor and the director of the mobility department had other ideas, but they never bothered to tell me what they were up to. One afternoon when I was in my mobility teacher's office, he told me that Mr. Dees, my guidance counselor, was in a meeting about plans to send me to Arkansas Enterprises for the Blind after I graduated from Perkins. Arkansas Enterprises is a rehabilitation school where you learned more about independent living. Now, I have nothing against schools of this type; I think they serve a purpose. But at this point in my life, I thought I was making an intelligent and rational decision to further my education at a college or university. It was bad enough that Mr. Dees felt he needed to meet with another Perkins administrator about my future, but worse than that, he had decided to do it behind my back.

I had just spent the better part of four years taking college preparatory courses, including two years of algebra, one year of geometry, one year of trigonometry, four years of Spanish, a year of history, a year of biology, a year of science, two years of computer, a year of physics, and four years of English, so now I was supposed to spend time in a rehab center a thousand miles from home? No way, pal!

When my mobility teacher told me what Mr. Dees was doing, he suggested that I confront Mr. Dees in his office. So I wasted no time, and managed to corner him before he went home that day. At this point, I would like to say something about my state of mind as I knocked at Mr. Dees' office door. During my eight years at Perkins, I dealt with two abusive housemothers, an unreasonable supervisor who wouldn't let me leave the kitchen, and several other unreasonable people, but never had I been so assertive with a member of the Perkins staff as I was the moment I sat down in one of Mr. Dees' chairs.

I told him that I had heard about his meeting, where the decision had been made to ship me to Arkansas, and I graphically told him exactly how I felt about that. I reminded him that I had the right to plan my own future, and that I already knew what that future was. Furthermore, he was never to go behind my back and make decisions for me without my knowledge. I laid into Mr. Dees so much that at the end of our conversation, he actually offered to walk me back to my cottage, something he had never done in the previous three years that I had known him.

The rumors about Arkansas suddenly came to an abrupt halt, as did my plans to go to a university. There was no connection, believe me. I merely decided that I would be better off at a junior college, and then with making the transition to a university later on. That's exactly what happened. I spent three years getting my Associate's degree in business administration at a local junior college, and then two additional years obtaining a Bachelor's degree in finance at the local university.

Chapter 23

Goodbye to Perkins

Throughout my Senior year in high school, which would be my last year at Perkins, I lived life from day to day, enjoying my friends and fulfilling my obligations without consciously realizing that this would be the last time I would be involved in these activities. It would be my last Christmas concert, my last drama club performance, my last group interaction on a field trip, my last socialization in the rec room, etc., yet I just lived life to the fullest. At one point, I even developed crushes on two girls months before leaving Perkins, not fully understanding that once I left, any potential relationships with these girls would be gone as well. But I suppose that when you live for the moment, you don't think ahead, because you're enjoying yourself. I found that I had more friends later in high school than I did during my first two or three years at Perkins, and that I was becoming more confident and outgoing.

As graduation approached, it was time to do what most Seniors in other schools would do in preparation for the big event, such as going to the Senior Prom, taking pictures for the yearbook, getting our caps and gowns, setting goals, and learning how to march down the aisle in Dwight Hall, where graduations were normally held. I didn't attend the Senior Prom, because I stuck to my own personal tradition of going home every weekend, a tradition I never broke during my eight years at Perkins. Though many of the students who could go home each weekend decided to stay at Perkins on occasion for various special events, I couldn't tear myself away from the desired constant in my life, which was home, sweet home, where I needed to spend quality time with my parents and other family members. I lived away from home five out of seven days each week, so the least I could do was go home at every opportunity. With that said, I had, and still have, many friends from Perkins, and I missed them the most of all once I left the campus permanently.

The students in my graduating class came from many different backgrounds and cultures. There were 10 of us, and though we got along well as a class, it was hard to say whether we'd all see one another again after graduation, given our different circumstances. I talked about Pedro, who was born and raised in Mexico City. I later learned that he returned there after spending a year in a Watertown apartment, even though that meant disrupting his solid relationship with his girlfriend. Without even asking Pedro how he would feel about leaving her once he graduated, I knew him well enough to predict his reaction. He would, and probably did, cry many tears, because it would have been impossible for the couple to remain together while she lived in Watertown and he in Mexico City.

Years later, I learned that Pedro found an apartment in Watertown and lived close to his girlfriend for one year after graduation, until parental intervention caused the two to break up. I don't recall whose parents interfered, but Pedro ultimately returned to Mexico to start a new life, a life that I am still trying to find out about as I search for him.

Moe is an Eskimo from Alaska. He spent five years at Perkins, until the day he graduated with us. He enjoys playing the guitar and was on the wrestling team. During our Junior year, Moe fathered a child with a Perkins sophomore during the mid–winter vacation, while staying at her parents' house. He went on to finish school, while the girl dropped out. It was later learned that she wanted to finish, but that the staff had a rather old–school attitude about it because of her pregnancy, despite the fact that she made all the necessary day care arrangements for the child in order to complete high school.

Juan was born in the Azores, but moved to America at a very young age. He quickly learned English and developed many friendships. I learned a lot from Juan, and was quite captivated by his analytical logic and creativity. Like me, Juan had a strong passion for math, science, and the computer. Today, he is working in the vending stand program somewhere near Boston.

After Jennie graduated with us, she continued with her passion for sports and athletics and joined Special Olympics. She was, and may still be, a rehabilitation counselor for the blind.

Trish pursued her music career, but died tragically at age 24 in her sleep. We never found out the cause, but we were saddened by the news, remembering how bright she was and how she loved to speak her mind about everything.

Pete is from New Jersey, and didn't attend Perkins until his Junior year. He was a member of the wrestling team and lived in the Community Living Program. Today, he is married and has decided to brush up on his computer skills.

Brent, who is from Maine, moved on to become a blind magician. He calls himself The Great Blindini.

James is from central Massachusetts. He was probably the quietist member of our class. However, just when I thought that James was extremely shy, I found out what a riot he was outside of class.

Mindy, a Jewish girl from Massachusetts, still lives close by. She enjoys going to Red Sox games and keeping in touch with old friends from the past.

As we all prepared for our final day as a class, after spending the better part of eight years together, I realized that our time together was about to come to an abrupt end. Several days before graduation, we were invited to spend an evening at Mr. Smith's house, as part of a tradition that all Seniors followed. Every year, the Senior class spent an evening with the director of Perkins during the last week of school. There was a house on campus where all directors lived during their administrations. While we were visiting Mr. Smith that evening, he made us feel very welcome. He offered us snacks, made small talk, thanked us for our contribution to Perkins, and talked with us about our futures. I won't speak for the rest of my class, but I know I felt very honored that the director of Perkins opened his door to us, whether or not it was a tradition for Seniors to visit him.

Graduation was fast approaching. On Wednesday, June 8, 1977, two days before the big event, we moved books and supplies as part of cleanup day. I recall the countless times I spent on the freight elevator that day with a small hand truck full of books. While several of us were rolling the hand truck along the corridors from one end of the Howe Building to the other, the principal decided to give me a book that would never be used at Perkins again. It was titled *Exploring the Moon.*

On Thursday, June 9, the student body had their usual Final Assembly, and when it was over, everyone except the Seniors and members of the chorus went home for the summer. Traditionally, the chorus stayed one extra day in order to sing at graduation, which always took place the day after summer vacation began for everyone else. To be truthful, I had never stayed that extra day, even though I was in the chorus for four years in Upper School. In previous years, once Final Assembly was over, I had packed up and gone home before anyone had a chance to question me as to why I wasn't going to participate in the chorus. Final Assembly marked the beginning of summer vacation, and when it was over, I had always felt that I needed to establish immediate closure and return home. I hadn't felt like staying one more day just so I could sing.

However, in my Senior year, things were a lot different. I was about to graduate from a school where I had spent eight years, and that was worth a lot to me. Of course I was going to stay an extra day for the graduation ceremony.

At my last Final Assembly, on June 9, 1977, I was given two awards, the Reginald Fitz award for scholarship, and the Drucker Award for English. I was very proud and honored, though I was extremely humble. When Final Assembly ended, everyone left for summer vacation except the Seniors, the members of the chorus, and several other students who had unusual travel problems.

By this time, it had become evident that we Seniors needed to think about bidding farewell to some very good friends, many of whom had spent years with us. While I began saying goodbye to those students who were neither graduating with me nor would be staying an extra day because they were members of the chorus, I thought of Pedro, because he was so emotional. Though I wouldn't have to say goodbye to him until the next day, I thought of the other friendships he had made at Perkins and the romantic relationship he had with his girlfriend. To be honest, I don't recall any final exchange between Pedro and his girl, but then again, I had no knowledge at the time that he had agreed to stay in a Watertown apartment for one year after graduation. The girl was several years older than Pedro, and she was at Perkins to brush up on her independent living skills. I did, however, notice the tears when he said goodbye to one or two close friends that afternoon.

Speaking of the afternoon before graduation, it was damp, cloudy, and very cold for June, but that didn't stop the remaining students from being invited to an outdoor picnic. We ate good food and told a lot of jokes, and in my case, I almost forgot about the next day and the future and lived for the exact moment. I refused to acknowledge that within 24 hours I wouldn't see these friends anymore.

That night was a normal night in the cottage, though the cottage seemed a bit more empty than usual, because a few students had already gone home for the summer. Needless to say, I cleared out my bureau and desk in my bedroom as I normally would before the start of all the other summer vacations, only this would be the last time. My suitcase was filled with my belongings, while my heart was filled with emotion.

The next morning, my last as a Perkins student, I woke up, had breakfast, and slowly prepared for the events of Graduation Day. My parents, though they didn't get along, were both going to attend the graduation ceremony as well as the luncheon beforehand. They would travel separately. Two other relatives would also be there to celebrate the day.

At approximately noontime, the graduating class and their families headed for the Northeast Building for their luncheon. We all introduced one another to as many of our relatives as we could. When the luncheon was over, our families went to Dwight Hall to wait for us while we had our class picture taken privately. Besides the fact that I was in the picture with nine of my classmates and to this day am proud of that picture, the other thing I can guarantee you is that I was the skinniest I would ever be again. From that moment on, I progressively gained weight.

It was now time for the graduation. Everyone in Dwight Hall watched as the graduates marched down the aisle to the stage. I was full of emotion, and I felt like crying at any moment. My world away from home for the past eight years was about to come to an end. As we sat on stage, we listened as the chorus sang a beautiful rendition of "No Man Is An Island." Jennie, our classmate, sang "Evergreen," the theme from *A Star is Born*, made popular by Barbra Streisand.

After the speeches were given and the diplomas handed out, it was time for us to leave the stage, walk out of Dwight Hall, and move forward with our lives. Before we left the Perkins campus for the last time, there was a receiving line for the graduates outside the Howe Building, where everyone would walk by to wish us good luck. This was it. It was the last time I would be with those with whom I had spent a lot of time over the years. I remember standing next to Pedro in line, and he and I both shed a lot of tears as we said goodbye to students and staff. Most of them would be back in the fall, but not us. We would be leaving our friends, our significant others, and our role models. It was one of the most emotional experiences I ever had in my entire life. I didn't seem to care that I was crying as each person shook my hand. At that moment, I didn't know when I would see these people again, if ever.

After we, the graduating class of 1977, left the receiving area, we all went our separate ways and proceeded to leave the Perkins campus. It was, for the most part, a fond farewell to the place which helped us develop into mature young adults. It was the place that offered Pedro romantic opportunities, gave him a chance to exploit his talents on the piano, and allowed him career development. It was the place that gave Jennie an opportunity to excel in athletics and other forms of leadership. It was the place that taught Juan what he needed to know so that he could become a terrific salesman. And finally, Perkins was the place that made all of us proud to have a quality education.

As I rode home with my family for the last time, knowing there would be no going back, I was, of course, happy to remain home, though I still had a very numb feeling about what had just transpired.

Though I was about to face life's challenges as a blind person outside of Perkins, I was happy with what I became as a result of my experiences at that school. I grew into somebody I liked, because I had the opportunities to pursue what I needed to pursue. Everything was accessible at Perkins. There were no barriers, forms of discrimination, political excuses, or anything else preventing me from achieving whatever I wanted to achieve. But now that I had graduated, it was a different story.

When people ask me what I liked about Perkins or what I gained from it, my answers are always the same. I made a lot of friends and received the best education possible, but through no fault of Perkins, I wasn't as ready to face life's challenges as a blind person as I would have liked.

I was also very happy that I was there at a time when change took place on campus, as Perkins evolved beyond its institutional reputation to being a school that promoted more freedom and independence. Not very many students could tell you that they attended Perkins during Mr. Smith's entire administration as director, while watching him change the environment almost at the snap of his fingers. Under Mr. Smith's leadership, where boys were concerned, girls went from being forbidden fruit to cottage mates. Also, of course, blindness wasn't always going to be the only issue that a Perkins student had. Consequently, Mr. Smith didn't allow you to wait until graduation to have work experience. He offered you career opportunities in high school. He allowed you to pave your own way toward independence, and he rewarded you with a key to your own cottage if you deserved it.

However, whatever Mr. Smith was, and however much of an effect he had or didn't have on the environment at Perkins, you were on your own once that cap and gown were put away. Now it was up to you to use your experience to the fullest in order to introduce yourself to a sighted world, where the sighted have most of life's advantages.

Furthermore, despite the moral, scholastic, and life education we received, most of the sighted world wouldn't understand the extent to which we blind people were capable of using our learned talents unless we showed them.

As the years went by, I reestablished old friendships and began to plan reunions. Today, I am happy to be among the Perkins circle once again, because these are some of the nicest people I have ever met, and I hope to remain in touch with them for the rest of my life.

The End

A Final Note of Appreciation

Leonore H. Dvorkin, of Denver, Colorado, proofread and edited this book.

Her husband, **David Dvorkin**, did the technical work necessary for its publication in print and e-book formats.

The Dvorkins are both prolific writers, with over 30 books and many essays and articles to their credit. Their son, Daniel Dvorkin, is also a writer. He has written two science fiction novels with his father, including a *Star Trek* novel.

David and Leonore invite you to visit their websites to learn more about their numerous publications.
David's website is **www.dvorkin.com**
Leonore's website is **www.leonoredvorkin.com**

One of Leonore's books is her account of her 1998 experience with breast cancer. The title is *Another Chance at Life: A Breast Cancer Survivor's Journey.* The second edition was published in 2012.

Also in 2012, the book was translated into Spanish by Gloria H. López. That title is *Una nueva oportunidad a la vida: El camino de una sobreviviente de cáncer de seno.*

Both books are available in print and e-book formats, and the English version is now available as an audiobook from

Audible.com. Three of David's novels are also available as audiobooks from Audible.

Since 2009, David and Leonore have been assisting other authors, both blind and sighted, with the writing and self–publishing of their own books.

For details of their editing and self–publishing services, see: **http://www.dvorkin.com/epubhelp/**

Made in the USA
Middletown, DE
30 August 2024